Irish Mythology for Teens

Enthralling Tales and Legends from Ancient Ireland

© Copyright 2025 - All rights reserved.

The content contained within this book may not be reproduced, duplicated, or transmitted without direct written permission from the author or the publisher.

Under no circumstances will any blame or legal responsibility be held against the publisher, or author, for any damages, reparation, or monetary loss due to the information contained within this book, either directly or indirectly.

Legal Notice:

This book is copyright protected. It is only for personal use. You cannot amend, distribute, sell, use, quote, or paraphrase any part, or the content within this book, without the consent of the author or publisher.

Disclaimer Notice:

Please note the information contained within this document is for educational and entertainment purposes only. All effort has been executed to present accurate, up-to-date, reliable, and complete information. No warranties of any kind are declared or implied. Readers acknowledge that the author is not engaging in the rendering of legal, financial, medical, or professional advice. The content within this book has been derived from various sources. Please consult a licensed professional before attempting any techniques outlined in this book.

By reading this document, the reader agrees that under no circumstances is the author responsible for any losses, direct or indirect, that are incurred as a result of the use of the information contained within this document, including, but not limited to, errors, omissions, or inaccuracies.

Free limited time bonus

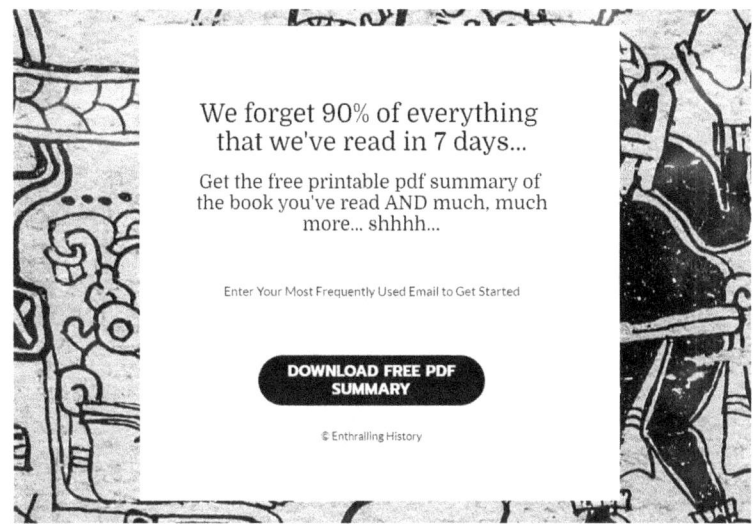

Stop for a moment. We have a free bonus set up for you. The problem is this: we forget 90% of everything that we read after 7 days. Crazy fact, right? Here's the solution: we've created a printable, 1-page pdf summary for this book that you're reading now. All you have to do to get your free pdf summary is to go to the following website: https://livetolearn.lpages.co/enthrallinghistory/

Or, Scan the QR code!

Once you do, it will be intuitive. Enjoy, and thank you!

Table of Contents

INTRODUCTION 1
CHAPTER 1: WHISPERS OF THE TUATHA DÉ DANANN.............................3
CHAPTER 2: TALES OF TÍR NA NÓG 15
CHAPTER 3: THE FIANNA CHRONICLES..22
CHAPTER 4: THE ULSTER CYCLE AND CÚ CHULAINN'S VALOR............30
CHAPTER 5: THE FLAME OF SAINT BRIGID..43
CHAPTER 6: THE MORRIGAN'S SHADOW 51
CHAPTER 7: DRUIDS AND MAGIC..60
CHAPTER 8: THE FENIAN CYCLE..72
CHAPTER 9: THE SECRETS OF THE SIDHE 83
CHAPTER 10: FOLKLORE AND LEGENDS AFTER CHRISTIANITY..........92
BONUS CHAPTER: LEGENDARY FIGURES IN IRISH HISTORY...............105
CONCLUSION 112
HERE'S ANOTHER BOOK BY ENTHRALLING HISTORY THAT
YOU MIGHT LIKE..115
FREE LIMITED TIME BONUS..116
BIBLIOGRAPHY 117
IMAGE SOURCES 119

Introduction

The mythology of most ancient peoples usually begins with a grand story of how everything came into being. There are many versions of Irish legends, myths, and folktales, but there isn't a creation myth. After the Irish became Christian, their old stories were rewritten to fit in with biblical stories, especially the Book of Genesis.

In this book, we will look at information from different sources, including modern pagans and interpretations written down by Christian monks. The monks and priests recorded the oral history of Ireland as it had been told for generation after generation.

What was sacred in Irish mythology was sinful in Christianity, so we can imagine the conflicting mindsets of those who first recorded the history of Ireland. Some tried to work the festivals and legends into Catholic narratives. They tried to teach the newly converted Irish people the error of their pagan beliefs and habits. However, the ancient myths and superstitions built into Irish culture stubbornly remained.

We are going to look at several stories from old manuscripts. Around the 11th century, one or more scholars put together previously recorded history and folktales in a manuscript called *Lebor Gabála Érenn* (*leh-vor gaw-baw-la ay-ren*), or *The Book of Invasions*. Many of the tales were transcribed from much older texts. Still, a chronological version of Irish mythology remained elusive.

Neither the monks nor historians could tell with certainty which stories and legends were based on real history and which were based on pure imagination. In addition, every tale has multiple versions, and some cross over with Scottish and Welsh tales.

When the Gaelic cultural revival started a few centuries ago, scholars sorted this jumbled legacy of myths and prehistory into four eras:

- The Mythological Cycle
- The Ulster Cycle
- The Fenian Cycle
- The Kings' Cycle

In this book, we will try to create a chronological version of events and people populating the mythological tales of Ireland. We will look at mysterious sounds and places that were explained through stories rooted in imagination. And through it all, we'll try to hold on to the charm of Irish storytelling, the wonder of ancient ideas, and the deep feelings that give these legends their lasting power.

Remember that there are **many** versions of the same heroes and stories in the mythology of ancient Ireland. So, do not be surprised when the same characters pop into several different stories!

Chapter 1: Whispers of the Tuatha Dé Danann

When the people who became known as the Irish settled in Ireland, they found traces of settlements left by older civilizations. Some of these were monumental stone structures, often overgrown by lush vegetation. Other strange places included mysterious standing stones with a large stone balanced crosswise on top. And then there were tunnels and great mounds of earth with stone or wood circles around them.

There were thick groves of beautiful trees and wild woods. The wind whistled eerily through these unknown places. Ancient gods and goddesses with the power to lift massive stones must have trodden this land, they thought. Where did they come from, and where did they go? Or were they still there? Any good imagination can conjure strange movements and beings in the shadows, especially in dark and unknown places. And so, the early Irish, the **Celts**, made up stories about these unknown beings that had come before them.

Arrival of the Tuatha Dé Danann, Ireland's Deities

It was the first day of summer. A thick fog rolled in from the west and covered the hills of the fair island of Innisfail. Some said it was a black cloud, and others swore it was white or grey.

When the mist lifted, it revealed a race of strikingly beautiful people. Their **ethereal** (*otherworldly*) beauty was emphasized by their lustrous pale skin. They looked like people who had hardly ever been in the sun. Some had long red hair; others were blonde. Piercing blue eyes and vivid green eyes took in the beauty of the land. They knew they had arrived in their forever home just as had been prophesied.

They were the people of the ancient mother goddess Danu. They were the Tuatha Dé Danann (*too-a day dah-nun*). They had traveled far across the cold, icy sea from the north. There, they had learned magic, wisdom, and many supernatural skills. Although they were not the first people on this green island, many of them would be revered as deities by later people because of their skills.

It is said that the roots of the Tuatha Dé Danann were from the most ancient race to have ever walked the earth. Their original homeland is unknown. That left room for many tales to be spun.

Ireland's mythology does not start with the creation of the earth like most cultures, nor do their deities or supernatural beings come from or live in the sky. Much later, the Catholic monks heard about the Tuatha Dé Danann from the Celts who lived in Ireland when the Romans were building their empire. The monks clarified the uncertainty of Ireland's origins for themselves and their followers by weaving them into the Catholic narrative. They stated that the Tuatha Dé Danann must have been the fallen angels cast out of heaven, which explains their supernatural skills and knowledge. Another explanation was that they were the children of Noah's son Japheth after the Great Flood.

The Tuatha Dé Danann roamed the earth for hundreds of years until they stopped at the four great cities of the four sages in the mysterious north. They learned from Senias (*see-nee-us*) in Murias (*mew-rius*) and from Morias (*moe-rius*) in Falias (*fi-lie-us*). In Gorias (*go-ri-us*), they learned from Urias (*you-rius*), and in Finias (*fee-nius*), they were taught by the poet Arias (*a-rius*).

When the Tuatha Dé Danann resumed their journey, they possessed the knowledge, powers, and skills learned from these sages. They also brought four magical treasures with them.

- **The Stone of Destiny** (*Lia Fáil* (*lee-uh fawl*) in Irish), which the Tuatha Dé Danann set down on the Hill of Tara. It was said it roared in recognition whenever a rightful king was crowned on it. The scrolls and marks on it are supposed to hold all the knowledge of the world.

Lia Fáil on the Hill of Tara in Ireland.[1]

- **The Spear of Victory**, which was held by Lugh (*loo*), a famous warrior. This spear made him invincible. It would find his prey, kill it, and then fly back to Lugh's hand.
- **A magic cauldron**, which was given to the Dagda, one of the leaders of the Tuatha Dé Danann. It always overflowed with food so that he could give to those in need.
- **The Sword of Destiny**, which was given to Nuada (*noo-a-da*), the first king of the Tuatha Dé Danann. It was lost to the Otherworld when King Nuada died in the Second Battle of Mag Tuired (*moy too-ruh*). There are whispers that a queen of the faeries stole it from Nuada in the Otherworld. She uses it to tempt humans with the promise that she will give it to them if they can fulfill three wishes for her.

The First Battle of Mag Tuired

The Fir Bolg (*feer bolg*), a hardworking agrarian people, were living in Ireland when the Tuatha Dé Danann arrived on the island. (**Agrarian people** cultivate the land, like farmers.) They had divided the land into five provinces. A king ruled over each province. One monarch was selected as the high king. He lived on the sacred Hill of Tara. The Tuatha Dé Danann asked them for part of the land, but the Fir Bolg refused.

This led to a mighty battle described in *The Book of Invasions*, or *Lebor Gabála Érenn* in Irish. Despite their powerful magic and superior skills, it took four days for the Tuatha Dé Danann to defeat the Fir Bolg. The surviving Fir Bolg were allowed to stay in the far western region of Ireland. The victors took over the rest.

The Fomorians

The Fomorians (*fo-mor-ee-ans*) were another mythological race living in Ireland before the Tuatha Dé Danann arrived. They were a nasty supernatural race of ugly one-eyed giants associated with chaos and disasters. Not all Fomorians were ugly, cruel monsters, though. Elatha, one of their kings, was good. He is described as darkly handsome in the Irish sagas. He was one of the few handsome Fomorians who intermarried with the Tuatha Dé Danann.

During a battle with the Fir Bolg, the king of the Tuatha Dé Danann, Nuada, lost his right hand. According to their customs, a disabled king could not rule. While someone worked on a replacement hand made of silver, a temporary king had to be appointed. The role fell to Bres. Bres was the son of a Tuatha Dé Danann woman, Ériu (*air-yu*), and the Fomorian king, Elatha.

Unfortunately, Bres inherited a nasty streak from his father's people. He was cruel and mean to his subjects. The Tuatha Dé Danann eventually kicked him out. By this time, Nuada's replacement arm, complete with new flesh that had been grafted over the silver, had fully healed. He became king of the Tuatha Dé Danann again.

The Fomorians by John Duncan.*

The Tuatha Dé Danann decided to rid themselves of the devilish Fomorians once and for all. War was brewing again because Bres had talked one of the Fomorian rulers into fighting with him to regain the Tuatha Dé Danann throne. Bres first tried to get his father, King Elatha, to help him, but this good king refused. So, Bres went to the evil Fomorians for help. Together, they gathered a mighty army. Nuada appointed Lugh as head of his army, and they met the enemy at Mag Tuired yet again.

In the Second Battle of Mag Tuired, a Fomorian king with a single yet deadly piercing eye, Balor of the Evil Eye, killed Nuada. Lugh killed Balor with a slingshot. His stone sent the evil eye flying out through the back of Balor's head into the midst of his soldiers. The eye killed Balor's soldiers when they looked into it. This allowed the Tuatha Dé Danann to win the battle. Lugh became king in Nuada's place.

Bres's life was spared on the condition that he teach the Tuatha Dé Danann how to plow, sow, and reap. When Lugh and two others of the Tuatha Dé Danann retrieved the magical harp of the Dagda from the fleeing Fomorians, their victory was complete.

The Last Invaders: The Milesians

According to some, the Milesians (*my-lee-zhuns*) are the ancestors of today's Irish people.

There are several theories of their ancestry, with some claiming they were descended from the Greeks, specifically from the region of Miletus. Miletus was home to some of the great Greek philosophers, such as Thales, Anaximander, and Anaximenes. Others claim they were Gaels, a branch of Celtic and Scythian heritage from the Spanish region of Iberia.

The Milesians on their way to Ireland.'

They invaded Ireland after the Tuatha Dé Danann reigned supreme for more than a century. Their arrival inevitably led to battles for supremacy of the land and culture. In folktales, the Tuatha Dé Danann selected a trio of sisters, Ériu, Banba, and Fodla, to negotiate peace on their behalf with the Milesians.

The Milesians selected their Druid prophet, Amergin (*a-mur-gin*), as their representative. They met on a hill called Uisneach (*ish-knock*) in the middle of the country. This hill has a special significance to the Irish since it stands at the intersection of all five ancient provinces.

The sisters had the gift of prophecy. Together, they made up a triple goddess. They realized that it was time for the Tuatha Dé Danann to move on to the realm of the Otherworld and for the Milesians to take over Ireland.

The sisters asked Amergin to name the land after them, knowing their race would always be remembered. Amergin was impressed by Ériu's stature and grace, so he selected her name. When the Milesians finally conquered the Tuatha Dé Danann, the land was called Éire (*air-uh*) in Irish. The Tuatha Dé Danann moved underground into the mystical Otherworld, where Tír na nÓg (*teer na nohg*), the land of Eternal Youth, was located, along with other mythological lands.

The Tuatha Dé Danann as depicted in John Duncan's The Riders of the Sidhe (1911).'

Pagans believe the Tuatha Dé Danann are still moving between our world and the Otherworld. They became known as faeries. These faeries must not be confused with the tiny, winged creatures we are familiar with. These are wingless spirits of all shapes and sizes. They vary from beautiful and kind to ugly, nasty trolls. The ancient Irish deities are among them.

Key Figures of the Tuatha Dé Danann

By the time the Christian monks started recording Irish mythology, particularly in relation to the Tuatha Dé Danann, these stories had been passed down for centuries. Many gods and goddesses had multiple roles, and some even overlapped. Here are just some from the lengthy list:

The Dagda – He was seen as a father figure, and some say he was the leader of the Tuatha Dé Danann. He was also a Druid. A Druid was like a priest and a sage, but we will talk more about them later. The Dagda could both give life and take it. He was also the god of fertility, agriculture, and wisdom.

He controlled time and the seasons. He was an exceptionally large man and was usually depicted with a pot belly, an unkempt beard, and a cloth around his head. Despite the Dagda's rough appearance, he was a protector. He was wise and shrewd and had an excellent sense of humor.

The Dagda had several children with two women of the Tuatha Dé Danann. He was a son of the mother goddess, Danu (*dah-noo*). Several of the tribes of Ireland claimed direct descent from

The winter solstice at Newgrange, Brú na Bóinne, where the Dagda lived.[5]

the Dagda. According to folklore, the Dagda lived at Brú na Bóinne (*broo na boy-na*), the seat of the famous tombs of Newgrange, Knowth, and Dowth.

The Dagda had three magic tools: a club that killed with one end and brought life with the other, a beautifully decorated magic harp made from oak with which he controlled time and the seasons, and a magic cauldron that was always filled with food for the hungry. He is also said to have had two pigs—one growing and one roasting. His orchards were always full of fruit.

According to one ancient Irish legend, the Dagda's harp was stolen by the Fomorians during a battle. After the harp was recovered by Lugh and the powers of light, it was said that the deities imbued it with powerful music that stirred the hearts of its listeners. People would weep in sorrow, laugh in joy, or fall into a restful sleep.

The Gaelic harp became the national emblem of Ireland. It has been displayed as a golden harp on a blue background since the 16th century. It is displayed today on the Irish presidential flag and is part of the Irish coat of arms.

- **Lugh** – He is also known as Lugh of the Long Arm because of his magic spear. When he stretched out his arm while holding his spear, it looked like one enormously long arm.

  Lugh was multi-talented. He was the god of arts and crafts of all kinds. He invented several games, including a board game named Fidchell, other ball games, and horse racing.

  He was a skilled and brave warrior. He could direct his magic spear at an enemy, knowing it would never miss and always return to him. He also owned a slingshot and a famous hound named Failinis (*fah-lin-ish*). Lugh is celebrated at the harvest festival of Lughnasadh (*loo-nuh-suh*) on the first day of August.

  Truth, oaths, and lawful kingship were part of Lugh's domain. Lugh was the father of one of Ireland's most revered folk heroes, Cú Chulainn (*koo kull-in*).

- **Ogma** – Ogma was the brother of the Dagda. He was the son of the mother goddess Danu. Ogma knew how to use language to persuade, **admonish** (*scold*), praise, explain, and charm. Have you heard the expression that someone has "the gift of gab" or that someone has "kissed the Blarney Stone?" That is Ogma's legacy!

- **Boann** – Boann (*boh-ahn*) was one of the Dagda's partners with whom he had children. She was the goddess of water and fertility.
- **Aengus** – He was a son of the Dagda and Boann. He lived at Newgrange. Aengus (*ayn-gus*) was skilled with words like his uncle Ogma. He is said to have been the god of love, summer, poetry, and youth. His verbal skills helped him win his inheritance and his wife.
- **Nuada** – Nuada was the first king of the Tuatha Dé Danann and the brother of the Dagda. He was a fair and just ruler. His people were elated when he returned to the throne after his magic healing following the loss of his hand in the First Battle of Mag Tuired.
- **Dian Cécht** – Dian Cécht (*dee-an kekt*) was the healer of the Tuatha Dé Danann. He replaced Nuada's hand so that Nuada could return to the throne. He was also known as the god of healing.
- **Brigid** – She was the goddess of healing. Brigid's other skills and knowledge were poetry and smithcraft. You can already see how these deities overlap! Brigid (*brih-jid*) also shares skills in arts and crafts with Lugh.
- **Délbaeth** – Délbaeth (*del-uh-vayth*) was a grandson of the Dagda, who succeeded him as the high king in some myths. If you are surprised that the Dagda, who was a Druid, was also a high king, that is because various sources add their own spin to the tales. Délbaeth was assassinated by his son Fiacha (*fee-uh-kha*), who wanted the kingship for himself.

The Children of Lir

One of the most famous stories from the time of the Tuatha Dé Danann is that of the children of Lir (*leer*). When Bodb (*buv*) Derg was made king of the Tuatha Dé Danann, Lir was angry because he felt that he was the better choice. He did not swear allegiance to the new king, which led to strife between the two. To appease Lir, Bodb offered him one of his daughters, Aoibh (*eve*), as his wife. Lir accepted, and there was peace at last between them.

Lir and Aoibh were incredibly happy together. They had a daughter and then a son and then twin sons. Unfortunately, Aoibh died soon after the birth of the twins. Lir, who really loved her by this time, grieved, but he was comforted by the love of his children.

After a while, Bodb offered Lir another of his daughters, Aoife (*ee-fuh*), as a bride. They were all happy with this arrangement. Aoife enjoyed the children and loved her new husband. However, this happy family relationship did not last. Aoife noticed her husband's deep love for his children and became jealous. She wanted all his love for herself.

Aoife set in motion a diabolical plan. She took the four children for a ride in her chariot. Then, she ordered her servants to kill them. If they did, they would be richly rewarded. They refused. She took a sword to kill the children herself, but she could not go through with it.

Instead of killing the children, she took them to a lake and told them to bathe. While they were in the water, she cast a spell on them that turned them into white swans. Lir's daughter was not afraid and asked her to put a time limit on the spell. She did not realize how evil the jealous queen was. Aoife said that the children would be in the same lake for three hundred years. Then, they would be in another colder lake for three hundred more years, and then they would live in the coldest of all the lakes for another three hundred years.

Aoife allowed them to keep their human speech. She said that they would be able to sing the most beautiful songs and that people from everywhere would come to listen. Afterward, Aoife returned to her father's court. When he asked why she did not bring the children with her, she said that Lir did not trust the children with Bodb Derg. He was suspicious and sent messengers to Lir to ask about Aoife's story. This was when Lir realized that Aoife had done something to his children. He learned the whole cruel story and let Bodb know about it. Bodb turned her into an air demon as punishment.

The lives of the swans got worse over the years since they were forced to move to ever colder lakes. At one lake, the water turned to ice, and their feet froze to the lake.

The story ends with the swans singing in a lake near a church. A monk looks after them by feeding them daily and listening to them. When the spell was broken at last, they turned into four incredibly old people. Saint Patrick was there just in time to baptize them into the Christian faith before they crumbled into dust.

Chapter 1 Activity

Circle the correct answer to the following questions. If you get stuck, the answers are in the back of the book!

1. What did the people who became known as the Irish find when they settled in Ireland?
    a) Gold and silver
    b) Traces of settlements left by older civilizations
    c) Modern buildings
    d) Deserted land
2. Who were the Tuatha Dé Danann?
    a) The first inhabitants of Ireland
    b) The people of the ancient mother goddess Danu
    c) The last invaders of Ireland
    d) The children of Noah's son Japheth
3. Who were the Fir Bolg?
    a) A race of one-eyed giants
    b) A hardworking agrarian race living in Ireland
    c) The ancestors of today's Irish people
    d) The children of the Tuatha Dé Danann
4. What is the Dagda known for?
    a) He was a cruel and unjust ruler.
    b) He was seen as a father figure.
    c) He was a warrior with a magic spear.
    d) He was the healer of the Tuatha Dé Danann.
5. What is unique about Lugh?
    a) He was known as Lugh of the Long Arm because of his magic spear.
    b) He was the king of the Tuatha Dé Danann.
    c) He was a son of the Dagda and Boann.
    d) He was the healer of the Tuatha Dé Danann.

Answers

1 (b)
2 (b)
3 (b)
4 (b)
5 (a)

Chapter 2: Tales of Tír na nÓg

In Irish mythology, there is a land of eternal youth, health, beauty, joy, and abundance. It is called Tír na nÓg (*teer na nohg*). Tír na nÓg is part of the Celtic Otherworld. The Otherworld is another world and is made up of different magical places. It is a place of magic where the spirits of the deities and the humans who have left the earthly realm mix together.

According to some interpretations, the Otherworld exists parallel to our world in a different but connected universe. There is only a thin veil between it and our world. Some compare it to the concept of life after death in paradise. It is considered a spiritual world. This is the place where the Tuatha Dé Danann moved to after the Milesians defeated them.

In many mythologies, time is in sync with our world. In Tír na nÓg, though, time moves very slowly. The inhabitants are eternally youthful. Some Otherworld folks can enter and leave our world at will. Some make themselves invisible while they are in our world. Their interactions with mortals can be benevolent or malicious.

Niamh Enters Tír na nÓg

One day, a beautiful young mortal girl named Niamh (*nee-uv*) receives a divine calling to the land of Tír na nÓg. She feels that this is her purpose—her destiny. She sets out on a magic horse provided by the fairy folk of Ireland and bridges the divide between this world and Tír na nÓg.

Niamh follows her instincts, which lead her through enchanted forests and lush green fields. She hears beautiful songs and meets all sorts of gorgeous creatures beyond human imagination. They radiate grace and beauty, living together in peace and perfect harmony with nature. Niamh discovers that there are many realms in this magical land. She visits the Hall of Eternal Youth. Next, she finds the Fields of Plenty, which are filled with mouthwatering fruits and a variety of beautiful flowers.

In another version of this legend, Niamh has always been an inhabitant of Tír na nÓg. She is one of the queens of the Tuatha Dé Danann.

The Sad Love Story of Niamh and Oisín

It was said that the inhabitants of Tír na nÓg often invited or tempted humans to their land. It was dangerous for humans to go there. Because of the timelessness in Tír na nÓg, a human visitor usually would never be able to return to their family and friends. Just a minute in the Otherworld could be years on earth.

When Niamh falls in love, it is with a young mortal hero. His father is Fionn, the leader of a band of famous warriors, the Fianna (*fee-uh-nuh*). Oisín (*uh-sheen*) is one of the bravest of these warriors, but his greatest talent is his poetry. Niamh invites him to her home in Tír na nÓg. Oisín joins her, promising his father that he will soon return to visit his homeland.

Despite their blissful life together, Niamh realizes after a while that Oisín misses his family and Ireland. She gives him her magic horse to cross the boundaries between the parallel worlds. But she warns him that he must make sure he does not touch the soil of Ireland. If he does, he will be unable to return to her. Oisín promises Niamh, the love of his life, that he will obey her instructions. He leaves after a loving embrace and returns to Ireland.

He immediately realizes that something is very wrong when he arrives. He does not recognize anybody or anything. When he asks where he can find his father, nobody knows who he is looking for. It is only when he asks some very old people that they recall who he is talking about—a long-dead hero from way back in the past!

Oisín is flabbergasted. To him, it felt like only a few days had passed, but he learned that in the normal world, three hundred years had come and gone! While he is sadly pondering his next move, he meets some men trying to lift a heavy stone from the ground. They ask for his help.

Mindful of Niamh's warning, Oisín makes sure that he stays on his horse. Unfortunately, the girth holding the saddle to the horse's back breaks, and he slips off the horse while lifting the stone. When his feet touch the ground, he immediately turns into a feeble and withered old man. Oisín realizes that he can never return to Niamh. He spends his last days telling people stories of the Fenian Cycle to Saint Patrick and others. They are known as the Ossianic Tales. He dies soon after.

While Oisín was living in Tír na nÓg, he became a popular storyteller of wonderful Irish folktales. He enthralled his listeners with stories of his life and adventures in the legendary band of warriors, the Fianna. Tales of the Fianna cross back and forth between mythology and history. Many of these stories could be true, while others incorporate the magic of mythology. The Fianna were even mentioned in records of old Irish law as the Fian!

Bran mac Febail Is Lured to Tír na nÓg

Another human who was lured to Tír na nÓg was King Bran mac Febail (*brawn mock fev-uhl*). One day, he falls into a trance-like sleep while walking in a forest. He suddenly hears beautiful music all around him, which lulls him to sleep. When he awakens, he sees a silver branch with white blossoms waving in front of his eyes.

He returns to his palace. There, he notices a strangely dressed woman among his companions. She tells him the branch is from an apple tree that grows in Emain (*eh-vin*), the Land of Women. He realizes that she is from the Otherworld. She sings him a song that tells all about the wonderful things in this land. It is a land of perfection, free from sickness and full of joy. She tells him to embark on a voyage to this land of beautiful women. Then, she disappears.

Bran prepares three groups of men to be led by three of his foster brothers. They all set sail to find this paradise. After two days, they are surprised and astonished to see a chariot approaching them over the water. It is Manannán (*mah-nuh-nawn*), the sea god. He explains that although they are sailing on an ocean, on his side of the veil, he is traveling across a field of flowers. Manannán tells Bran that he will have a son in Ireland in his absence. He predicts that the voyagers will reach their destination that evening.

A short while after this encounter, Bran stops their boat at an island. The people do not seem to hear their greetings from the ship, so Bran sends a scout to find out why all the people on the shore are laughing nonstop. The scout joins them in their laughter, and Bran is forced to leave him behind.

Soon after this, they arrive at their destination, the Land of Women. When Bran hesitates to stop, the women's leader throws a magic ball of twine, which sticks to his hand and allows her to pull their ship ashore. All the men quickly find companions for themselves. Bran goes off with the leader. They feast and make merry for what they think is one year.

At last, the women allow them to leave, but their leader warns them not to set foot on Irish soil. When they arrive on Ireland's shores, Bran calls out his name to let the people know he is back. But nobody recognizes his name or any of the men. When one man jumps off the boat, he turns to dust as soon as his feet touch the ground. Bran realizes what has happened. They had all been warned about the passing of time in the normal world.

Bran and his men told their story from their ship to the listeners onshore. Some versions say they also handed them a fully detailed record written in the Ogham (*ow-uhm*) script. Then, they said farewell and sailed away forever. The Ogham script was a script developed around the 4th century CE. It was used until about the 6th century to write Old Irish.

Mythical Lands in Ireland's Mythology

In some legends of the Tuatha Dé Danann, their new domain after the Milesians took over lay to the west of Ireland. There is a legend that an island existed—and some believe it still exists—to the west of Ireland. Cartographers of the Middle Ages drew such an island on maps as early as the 14th century. The most common name for it is Hy-Brasil.

Two of Ireland's saints also visited the island, and they each gave a description of it that was almost identical. It was described as an island of plenty, its people filled with joy and laughter. Both called it a "promised land." Saint Brendan, who was known as a navigator and voyager, described it as the "Isle of the Blessed."

Sometimes, the island was said to be visible southwest of Galway Bay, and at other times, it was visible from the shores between County Cork and County Antrim. It is clear from the legends that it was believed to be an island that not only rose and sank beneath the waves but also moved up and down the coast!

Tír na nÓg was one of the island's names in tales as old as the 7th century. Its lasting fascination is that it has been witnessed to appear and then vanish according to some old legends. Some say that it disappears under the waves for seven years and then reappears for a brief time. It was often described as very green with purple mountains.

Later, a famous story was told that said Captain Nesbitt of County Donegal was sailing in the Atlantic to the southwest of Ireland one day when a heavy fog suddenly enveloped his ship. When the fog lifted, they were dangerously near rocks and could see the island a little way off.

Four of the sailors rowed there. They explored the island and returned with silver and gold. They said that an old man living there had given it to them.

Many years later, Roderick O'Flaherty visited the island. He also met the old man. His name, according to O'Flaherty, was Morogh (*muh-ruh*) O'Ley, who said that he had been on the island for only two days. Does that not sound suspiciously like the way time passes in Tír na nÓg?

The Lost City of Kilstiffen

The legends of Ireland change and get mixed up over time. There could be a connection between Hy-Brasil and the lost city of Kilstiffen (*kill-stiff-en*). In one legend, this city rises above the waves below the Cliffs of Moher every seven years, just like Hy-Brasil rises every seven years. They are both situated, like Tír na nÓg, off the west coast of Ireland.

It is said that Kilstiffen is the most beautiful city. It rests on pillars of gold. The rooftops of the palaces are made of gold. In fact, it has gold roofs everywhere, from the churches to the towers. The streets are perfectly laid out.

According to legend, the city sank beneath the waves when the king lost or misplaced the golden key to the city's gate during a battle. Some say that if you stare long enough into the waters when the sea is calm, you can see the shiny city in the depths of the Atlantic Ocean. It will rise and stand on the land again only when the key is found. Of course, that has not happened yet!

The legends of Tír na nÓg and other magical places embody all the elements of paradise. It is an afterlife filled with joy, health, eternal youth, and happiness. As such, it is used in stories, books, films, and video games by artists, authors, and filmmakers to this day.

Chapter 2 Activity

Can you answer the following questions?

1. What is Tír na nÓg?

___

___

___

2. Who is Niamh, and what is her connection to Tír na nÓg?

___

___

___

3. Why does Oisín leave Tír na nÓg, and what happens when he returns to Ireland?

___

___

___

4. What is the common name of the island that is believed to exist to the west of Ireland, according to legends of the Tuatha Dé Danann and medieval cartographers?

___

___

___

5. How is time believed to pass in the land of Tír na nÓg?

___

___

___

Answers

1. Tír na nÓg is a land in Irish mythology known for its eternal youth, health, beauty, joy, and abundance. It exists parallel to our world in a different but connected universe.
2. Niamh is a young mortal girl who receives a divine calling to the land of Tír na nÓg. She travels there on a magic horse provided by the faerie folk of Ireland.
3. Oisín leaves Tír na nÓg because he misses his family and Ireland. When he returns to Ireland, he finds that three hundred years have passed, and he cannot recognize anybody or anything.
4. The mystical island west of Ireland was called Hy-Brasil.
5. Time passes much more slowly in Tír na nÓg than in the normal world, so it seems to be a land of eternal youth. A mere minute in the Otherworld could represent hundreds of years in our world.

Chapter 3: The Fianna Chronicles

If you grew up in Ireland or an Irish community somewhere in the world, chances are that your bedtime stories included legends of the Fianna and the great folk hero Fionn mac Cumhaill (*fyun mac coo-ull*; most English speakers say Finn mac Cool). Fionn was the last leader of a band of warriors called the Fianna. They roamed Ireland as protectors of the people.

The Fianna

The period in which the Fianna operated came to be known as the Fenian Cycle in Irish mythology. According to one legend, the Fianna lived off the land during summer by hunting and foraging. They were housed and fed by the elite during winter in payment for their services to protect law and order in the land.

The Fianna was created by the third high king of Ireland, Cormac mac Airt (*art*), in the 3rd century CE. The main stories of the Fianna come from the clans of Leinster under the leadership of Cumhaill and Connacht under the leadership of Goll mac Morna. Their purpose was to protect the people from threats, crime, and invasions.

How to Join the Fianna

Members of this elite group of warriors were carefully selected from the best of those who asked to join them. After all, they were the guardians of the people and the land and answered to the high king himself. It was a prestigious achievement, and they were greatly admired by the people.

The young applicants were given a series of challenges to test their courage, physical and mental strength, and character. They were also tested for their tracking, hunting, and survival skills. Intelligence and knowledge tests required that applicants know twelve books of poetry. These poems detailed the genealogy, history, and legends of Ireland.

Only those with the best skills and the highest sense of duty, honor, chivalry, and wisdom would become a Fian. They had to swear an oath of allegiance to their comrades and their leader. Once a man was accepted and had sworn the oath, he was a Fian for life. Those who wanted to leave were seen as traitors.

The original Fianna included several groups of men. However, in later sagas, there appears to have been only one united band of warriors. Most of the tales and legends revolve around their last leader, Fionn mac Cumhaill, the son of Cumhaill.

The Birth of Fionn mac Cumhaill

Cumhaill fell in love with Muirne (*moor-nuh*), the daughter of a Druid. Her father forbade her to marry, so Cumhaill abducted her. The high king sent troops, including the Fianna of Goll mac Morna, to bring the couple back. Goll mac Morna killed Cumhaill in the Battle of Cnucha (*noo-kha*). They returned the pregnant Muirne to her father, who wanted to kill her. Luckily, the high king intervened and sent her to Cumhaill's sister and her husband.

Cumhaill's sister was a Druidess named Bodhmall (*bode-wal*). She and her friend, Liath Luachra (*lee-uh loo-uh-kra*), raised the son that was born of the union between Cumhaill and Muirne. Liath Luachra was a famous and fearsome warrior, and she taught the boy to be a great warrior. Bodhmall educated and trained him in life skills and how to be honorable. This boy became the famous Fionn mac Cumhaill.

The Salmon of Knowledge

The Salmon of Knowledge.⁶

Fionn mac Cumhaill gained most of his knowledge and wisdom from a supernatural source. His two foster mothers enrolled him as an apprentice with a famous bard named Finnegas. One day, while they were relaxing by the River Boyne, Finnegas told Fionn that an old Druid had once told him that there was a magic fish in the river.

That fish was the Salmon of Knowledge. The old Druid had told Finnegas that the salmon ate hazelnuts from a magic tree on its banks. The Druid believed that the first person who could catch and eat the salmon would gain all the knowledge in the world.

The old poet said that he had tried to find that fish for many years. Then, one day, when he and Fionn were sitting by the river staring into its waters, Finnegas saw the salmon. He dived into the water, clothes and all, and caught the fish. He gave the fish to Fionn to cook while he went back to his house, presumably to change into dry clothes.

Soon, the large fish was cooking on a stone set over a small fire. The poet had told Fionn that he was not allowed to taste even a morsel of it.

As the pink flesh started to sizzle on the stone, Fionn decided to turn the fish so that it would cook evenly on both sides. His left thumb accidentally slipped off the fish and was burned on the hot stone.

He immediately stuck his sore thumb in his mouth. He quickly realized that his finger was full of oil from the fish. He felt a strange surge of energy. When he gave the fish to Finnegas, the old poet saw a difference in Fionn. He asked what had happened, and Fionn told him the truth.

Finnegas knew that the fish oil had transferred all its knowledge to Fionn. He gave him the whole fish to eat and watched closely. But it was only when Fionn stuck his left thumb into his mouth that all that wisdom and knowledge returned. In the future, if Fionn needed knowledge of anything, all he had to do was stick his left thumb in his mouth!

Fionn mac Cumhaill, Leader of the Fianna

Fionn mac Cumhaill, the leader of the Fianna.[7]

After Fionn mac Cumhaill proved himself physically and mentally superior in the grueling tests to join the Fianna, the high king appointed him as its leader. Some versions of the story say that Goll mac Morna simply handed over leadership to him after realizing that Fionn would be a better leader than he was.

Another story goes that Fionn killed a nasty supernatural harpist, Aillen (*ahl-yen*) the Burner, who was one of the fairy folk from the Otherworld. Aillen cast a sleeping spell on everybody on the Hill of Tara at Samhain (today's Halloween) with his music. Only Fionn was not affected, so he was able to kill him. The high king was so pleased to be rid of the pesky harpist that he rewarded Fionn mac Cumhaill with the leadership of the Fianna.

Fionn's Love Interest

One day, Fionn was hunting with his dogs, Bran and Sceolang (*sko-lung*). When he caught a deer, his dogs prevented him from killing it. He took it to his camp instead. That night, the deer turned into a beautiful woman. Her name was Sadhbh (*sive*). It turns out that she had been turned into a deer by the spell of a Druid whose love she had **spurned** (*rejected*). The safety of Fionn's camp turned her back into a woman. Of course, they fell in love and were soon married!

After a while, Fionn had to leave to deal with invaders who had crossed into Ireland. Fer Doirich (*far dor-ik*), a Druid, disguised himself as Fionn and lured Sadhbh away from camp. As soon as she left the camp, the spell returned.

Upon Fionn's return, he searched everywhere for her. All he found in the forest where he had originally met her as a deer was a little boy wandering around. He had been raised by a deer. Fionn knew that it was his son. He named him Oisín. Oisín became a famous bard. Yes, this is the same Oisín from the story of Tír na nÓg! But Sadhbh was forever lost to Fionn.

The Battle of Gabhra or "Cath Gabhra"

The high king who had created the Fianna, King Cormac mac Airt, was succeeded by his son, Cairbre Lifechair (*kahr-bruh lif-er-khar*). He had a beautiful daughter who was engaged to a prince of the Déisi (*day-shee*). The Déisi were renters who paid landowners and kings for the use of their land.

Two sons of Cairbre Lifechair murdered the prince before the ceremony. The Déisi refused to pay the dowry, of which the Fianna would have received a large share from their king.

This was when the Fianna lost their honor and prestige. Fionn mac Cumhaill and his warriors still demanded their share from the high king, Cairbre Lifechair. He was furious because he realized that the Fianna were no longer serving and protecting their country with pure intentions. Over the years, they had amassed too much power, wealth, and glory. They had become arrogant, as so often happens when a person or group gains too much power.

The king called up a huge army from across Ireland. According to some sources, the forces gathered at Gabhra (*gow-ra*) near the Hill of Tara. The Fianna was wiped out, and the battle ended when Fionn mac Cumhaill was killed. The only two left were Fionn's son Oisín and Caoilte mac Ronan (*keel-cha mac roh-nawn*). They traveled the land, telling the stories of the Fianna.

Remember Oisín from the story of Tír na nÓg? He died upon returning to our world to visit his father. He found his father and the Fianna were long gone. This is a typical example of how myths become mixed up when several writers record oral history from different sources.

The Legacy of the Fianna

Tales of the heroism, courage, loyalty, and integrity of the Fianna set the stage for Irish nationalism throughout the ages. These are ideals Irish people hold close. In their quest for independence, these ideals have at times been twisted or neglected. Other times, they have brought out the most admirable qualities of human nature.

Chapter 3 Activity

Can you answer the following questions?

1. What were the requirements for joining the Fianna?

2. Who was Fionn mac Cumhaill, and how did he become the leader of the Fianna?

3. Describe the story of the Salmon of Knowledge.

4. Who was Sadhbh, and what was her relationship with Fionn mac Cumhaill?

5. What led to the Battle of Gabhra, and what was the outcome?

6. Why did the Fianna lose their honor and prestige?

Answers

1. Members of the Fianna were carefully selected from the best of those who asked to join them. The young applicants were given a series of challenges to test their courage, physical and mental strength, and character.
2. Fionn mac Cumhaill was the son of Cumhaill. He became the leader of the Fianna after proving himself in the grueling skills and endurance tests to join the Fianna.
3. The story of the Salmon of Knowledge tells how Fionn mac Cumhaill gained all the knowledge and wisdom in the world from eating a special salmon.
4. Sadhbh was a woman who had been turned into a fawn by the spell of a Druid. Fionn mac Cumhaill fell in love with her, and they got married.
5. The Battle of Gabhra was caused by a dispute over a dowry. The Fianna was wiped out, and the battle ended when Fionn mac Cumhaill was killed.
6. The Fianna lost their honor and prestige when they demanded their share of a dowry from the High King Cairbre Lifechair. He realized that the Fianna were no longer serving and protecting their country with the pure intentions of their oath.

Chapter 4: The Ulster Cycle and Cú Chulainn's Valor

The next cycle in Irish mythology is known as the Ulster Cycle. It dates to around the 1st century CE, according to some interpretations. Tales from this cycle concentrate on the trials and tribulations of the greatest hero of Ulster, Cú Chulainn (*koo kull-in*). In the entangled Irish world of myth and history, it is impossible to know if Cú Chulainn was a real person. However, it is possible this hero was based on a historical figure despite his supernatural traits and achievements.

The king of Ulster in the northeast of Ireland, Conchobar mac Nessa

Cú Chulainn, ancient Ireland's greatest hero.'

(*kon-kur-vur mac ness-uh*), had a special private army. They were known as the Knights of the Red Branch. Cú Chulainn was their most famous warrior.

Cú Chulainn was magically conceived when his mother, Deichtine (*deck-tin-uh*), drank water and accidentally swallowed a tiny creature in it. Deichtine was the sister of King Conchobar mac Nessa. It was whispered that Cú Chulainn's father was Lugh, who was of the ancient mystical race of the Tuatha Dé Danann. Similar to other mythological heroes, since Cú Chulainn had a human as one parent and a deity as the other, he was considered a demigod.

In another version of Cú Chulainn's conception, Deichtine and the Ulstermen are caught in a heavy rainstorm. They find shelter with a couple in a house that suddenly appeared out of the gloom. During the night, Deichtine helps the woman deliver her baby. When dawn breaks, the rain stops, and the house and the couple suddenly disappear. Soon after, Deichtine finds that she is miraculously pregnant. Lugh appears to her in a dream and reveals that he is the father of her baby. He instructs her to name the baby Setanta.

Cú Chulainn fulfilled an old prophecy in Ireland that said a great warrior would be born one day whose life would be full of conflict and outstanding **valor** (*courage*). Some versions say a Druid prophesied at his birth that his deeds would give him eternal fame but that his life would be short.

Cú Chulainn's mother named him Setanta (*seh-tan-tah*) as Lugh had instructed her.

In some versions of Irish mythology, Cú Chulainn was very handsome and muscular. Over time, some abnormal features were added to his appearance, but he remained handsome and attractive to women. However, according to these myths, he had seven fingers on his hands and seven toes on his feet to increase his agility. They also said that he had seven pupils in each eye, which made his vision better than anyone else's.

In another, more mortal genealogy of Setanta recorded in Old Irish in the Ulster Cycle, the author of *Compert Con Chulainn* (*The Conception of Cú Chulainn*) concludes that Cú Chulainn's parents were Deichtine and Sualtam mac Róich. In this version, Deichtine is the daughter of the king of Ulster, Conchobar mac Nessa, rather than his sister.

One day, the young Setanta was invited to a feast at the house of the blacksmith, Culann. He was attacked by Culann's guard dog. As small as he was, Setanta already showed remarkable strength. He killed the menacing dog even though he was only seven years old. To **placate** (*calm*) Culann, he offered to act as his dog until it could be replaced. Thus, his name became Cú Chulainn, which means "dog of Culann," for the rest of his life.

Setanta killed the blacksmith's Irish Wolfhound.'

Cú Chulainn was given exceptional and magical talents by the deities. These included skills in magic, poetry, warfare, and wisdom. Cú Chulainn received training from Scáthach (*skaw-hakh*), a renowned warrior woman in Scotland. She honed his fighting skills. She taught him how to use his magic spear, Gáe (*gay*) Bulg, which she had given to him.

While in Scotland, Cú Chulainn fought against Scáthach's sister, Aífe (*ee-fa*), who was a rival of Scáthach. After he triumphed over Aífe, they entered into a relationship. Cú Chulainn and Aífe had a son together and named him Connla. Connla had a heartbreakingly tragic end, which we will get into later.

Cú Chulainn's Superhuman Gifts

Cú Chulainn received supernatural powers from his father, Lugh. His wisdom, for example, was not only beyond his years but also surpassed normal human wisdom. His mortal qualities could all be described as beyond those of an ordinary human.

Here are some of the ways that made Cú Chulainn stand out from other humans:

- Gáe Bulg was Cú Chulainn's magic spear. It caused a person's death by tearing open the inside of even the smallest wound it inflicted. Gáe Bulg was gifted to him by his trainer, Scáthach.

- When Cú Chulainn was in a battle rage, he transformed into an undefeatable supernatural monster. Every muscle in his body would bulge, his teeth were bared, his mouth would enlarge, and some said he could even breathe fire. He also had unbelievable speed. He was unbeatable. This transformation was called *riastrad* (*ree-uh-strahd*).

- He was an outstanding poet who could bring his audience to tears or laughter. After he was forced to kill his beloved foster brother in a battle, he composed a moving poem that was passed down orally. It was later recorded in the Book of Leinster.

- He displayed chivalry and wisdom far beyond his years since childhood.

- Cú Chulainn was fearless and unbeatable in battle, regardless of the number of enemies he faced.

Cú Chulainn's Taboos (Geas)

Cú Chulainn was forbidden to commit certain acts. One was that he should never eat dog meat. The second one was that he must never refuse hospitality. He had to always accept food offered to him by a woman. If he broke one of these **taboos** (*forbidden actions*), the consequences would be devastating. It could even bring about his death.

The Love Story of Emer and Cú Chulainn

When Cú Chulainn was still very young, he fell in love with Emer, the second daughter of King Forgall of Lusk. The king would not allow him to woo Emer. In their local tradition, his eldest daughter had to marry first. King Forgall also did not like Cú Chulainn or his lack of reputation at that time.

So, King Forgall disguised himself as an old sage and went to Ulster to persuade Cú Chulainn to go to Scotland to be trained by Scáthach and build himself a reputation first. Cú Chulainn accepted this challenge. King Forgall hoped that the training and adventures of such a trip would make Cú Chulainn forget Emer or even get himself killed. After Cú Chulainn returned some years later, the king still refused.

This time, he set a series of tasks for Cú Chulainn to complete before he would be accepted as a suitor. The tasks he set were impossible for any man. In the meantime, it was said that Ulstermen searched all over Ireland to find another bride for Cú Chulainn because his masculinity and striking appearance caused issues.

Poems about Cú Chulainn tell us that women loved him. The women in Ulster would even climb over their menfolk just to get a glimpse of him because he was so handsome and famous.

Cú Chulainn insisted that Emer was the only woman suitable for him. She was beautiful. She had a lovely voice, a clever mind, wisdom, and purity. Cú Chulainn completed the tasks that the king had set for him with great success because of the help of his father, Lugh, and the training he had received from Scáthach.

When Forgall still refused, Cú Chulainn grew angry. He killed twenty-four of Forgall's warriors and abducted Emer. He also stole the king's treasure. In the chaos that followed, Forgall fell off his balcony and died. Luckily, Emer forgave Cú Chulainn for causing her father's death, and they finally got married.

Táin Bó Cuailnge or the Cattle Raid of Cooley

In Connacht, Ireland, the king and queen were comparing their personal riches. The king won this little contest because he owned a magnificent white bull. The proud queen, Medb, also called Maeve, could not stand the thought of this. There was only one bull in Ireland that could outshine that of the king: the brown bull called Táin (*tawn*) of the Ulaids (*ull-ids*) of Cooley in Ulster. The queen resolved to raid their cattle to get the bull!

The bulls of Connacht and Ulster.[10]

The legend is known as the *Táin Bó Cúailnge* (*tawn Bow koo-lin-ya*), which means the "Cattle Raid of Cooley." The queen used a magic spell to put the warriors of Ulster to sleep. Because Cú Chulainn was not born in Ulster, the spell had no effect on him. He went into battle and transformed himself into his monster persona. He stormed into the ranks of Medb's army like a killing machine.

Then, he challenged Medb to pit her champions against him. She agreed, and they came at him one by one at the different fords of the river. He killed them, one by one!

In a pause between the battles, he met the Morrigan of the Tuatha Dé Danann. She came to him as a beautiful young woman. He spurned her advances since the battle was not over yet. He learned later that this young woman was the Morrigan—a goddess to be wary of. The Morrigan prophesied that he would die young. She told him that she would be there at his death.

Meanwhile, Medb had another trick up her sleeve. Although it is not explicitly stated in the legend, Medb could have been the same Medb mentioned in the myths of the Tuatha Dé Danann. She stirred up jealousy against Cú Chulainn in the heart of his best boyhood friend and foster brother, Ferdiad (*fair-dee-ud*), who was one of the warriors from Connacht. The two ended up fighting each other. The battle raged for several days. Ferdiad and Cú Chulainn fought with their comrades and each other during the day. At night, they would nurse each other's wounds and swear to their everlasting brotherly love.

Mural in Dublin of Cú Chulainn fighting Medb's champions.[11]

Ferdiad was eventually killed by Cú Chulainn. Medb's army was beaten. The queen had to flee the battle and was pursued by the Ulstermen. Cú Chulainn displayed his chivalry by protecting her during her retreat because he saw how broken and sad she looked.

The Tragic Death of Aífe's Only Son

Connla, the son of Cú Chulainn and Aífe, Scáthach's sister, grew up in Scotland with his mother. His father left Scotland before he was born. His mother told him about his father's training with Scáthach, and Connla followed in his footsteps. He was still very young when he left Scotland to search for his father in Ireland.

Another version of the story says that Cú Chulainn gave Aífe a thumb ring. He told Aífe to send Connla to Ireland as soon as the ring fit him. He left Aífe with three taboos to pass on to his son when he was old enough to understand. Connla was not allowed to turn back once his journey started. He was never to refuse a challenge. And he was not allowed to tell anyone his name when he came to Ireland.

Legend has it that Connla arrived in Ireland in a bronze boat with golden oars. As a stranger, he was challenged by some of the young warriors in Ireland. He quickly overcame them. Cú Chulainn was called in to defeat him. Connla could not tell Cú Chulainn who he was, so he had to fight his father.

Connla fought bravely, but in the end, Cú Chulainn used the Gáe Bulg to wound him. With his last breath, Connla sighed that together they could have conquered the whole world. With a broken heart, Cú Chulainn recognized him and told his comrades that the young man was his son.

Cú Chulainn and the Faerie

It is said that the love between Emer and Cú Chulainn ran deep. Emer knew that Cú Chulainn had a wandering eye for beautiful women, but she was never jealous because he loved her more. Well, except for one.

Fand, the beautiful wife of the god of the sea, Manannán, was left alone by her husband. The Fomorians saw this as their chance to take over the Irish Sea. Three of them attacked Fand, and she pleaded with Cú Chulainn to help her defend her domain. Cú Chulainn agreed on the condition that Fand marry him. At this time, the two had never even met in person. But Fand had no choice. She agreed to the deal, and they successfully defended her domain.

As soon as Cú Chulainn and Fand met in person, they fell in love with each other. Manannán knew that the relationship could only lead to catastrophe. Fand was a faerie, and Cú Chulainn was a mortal. Plus, he was already married to Emer.

Emer was devastated. She planned to kill Fand. But when she saw how great Fand's love for Cú Chulainn was, she could not go through with her plans. She wanted her beloved to be happy, and if that meant giving him up to Fand, she would do so. When Fand found out about Emer's selflessness, she realized that Cú Chulainn belonged with Emer, and she returned to Manannán.

Cú Chulainn, Emer, and Fand.[13]

Cú Chulainn and the Hag

Because Cú Chulainn was so attractive, many women fell in love with him. There is a legend about an ugly old witch who fell madly in love with him. Mal refused to accept his rejections. She stalked him wherever the Knights of the Red Branch went.

Eventually, her infatuation became such a problem that Cú Chulainn had to leave his comrades and flee since his code of honor prevented him from killing the old hag. She did not even get tired. The excitement of the chase seemed to make her full of energy. Mal chased him all across Ireland.

At the mouth of the River Shannon lay the magnificent Cliffs of Moher, with Diarmuid and Grainne's Rock (*deer-mid* and *grawn-ya*) close by in the turbulent waters off the coast. After arriving there, Cú Chulainn made a plan. Mal was old, so if he could leap from the top of the cliffs across the waves onto the rock, she surely could not come after him. So, that is what he did.

Unfortunately for Cú Chulainn, a breeze blowing from the land to the sea helped Mal make the jump successfully! Cú Chulainn quickly made the jump back to land. This time, Mal did not make it because she was jumping against the wind's direction. She splattered all over the rocks below the cliffs, her blood turning the waters of the bay red.

The small bay was named Malbay, and the rocks became known as Hag's Head because some people swore that if the light was exactly right, you could see Mal's face in them.

Death of Cú Chulainn

Throughout his many battles and relationships with women, Cú Chulainn made many enemies. One legend says that another champion warrior, Lugaid mac Con Roí (*loo-uhd mac kun roh-ee*), was one of these enemies. He hated Cú Chulainn with a passion because Cú Chulainn had an affair with his mother and killed his father.

Lugaid got together with other enemies of Cú Chulainn, and they conspired to trick Cú Chulainn into breaking his taboos to make him vulnerable. Cú Chulainn accepted a plate of food offered to him by an old woman. (Did you remember that one of his taboos was never to refuse food offered by a woman?) By not breaking this taboo, Cú Chulainn broke another taboo: never to eat dog meat.

Cú Chulainn's body had already been wounded during the fighting, but Cú Chulainn's spirit was now weakened. Meanwhile, Lugaid had three special spears made. The spears were prophesied to kill three kings. The group of enemies met Cú Chulainn in battle. Lugaid threw his first spear at Cú Chulainn, but he deflected it with his shield, and it killed his charioteer instead. The next one killed one of his chariot horses. The third spear hit him in the stomach, leaving a gaping wound. His guts started to spill out.

The legend tells us that even in the face of death, Cú Chulainn displayed extraordinary courage. He pressed his innards back into his body, tied himself to a standing stone, and beckoned his enemies to approach. They were still afraid of him, and they could not see if he was still alive. Only when the Morrigan perched on his shoulder in the guise of a raven did they know he was dead. Lugaid stormed closer to behead him.

One of Cú Chulainn's friends had sworn that if the hero died before he did, he would avenge his death before sunset on the same day. This warrior, Conall the Victorious, raced after Cú Chulainn's enemies and killed Lugaid, taking his head in revenge.

It was recorded much later by the Catholic monks that Cú Chulainn's soul visited the queens of Ulster that night singing a mystical song in which he foretold the coming of Christ and Armageddon.

Statue of the dying Cú Chulainn in a post office in Dublin.[18]

Chapter 4 Activity

Answer the questions below.

1. What is the Ulster Cycle in Irish mythology, and who is its main hero?

___

___

___

2. What is the meaning of Cú Chulainn's name, and how did he get it?

___

___

___

3. Who trained Cú Chulainn, and what skills did he acquire from her?

___

___

___

4. What are some of Cú Chulainn's superhuman gifts, and how did he use them?

___

___

___

5. How did Cú Chulainn's life end, and what role did his taboos play in his death?

___

___

___

Answers

1. The Ulster Cycle is a cycle in Irish mythology that dates to around the 1st century CE. The tales from this cycle focus on the trials and achievements of the greatest hero of Ulster, Cú Chulainn.
2. The name Cú Chulainn means "dog of Culann." He got this name after he killed Culann's guard dog and offered to act as his dog until it could be replaced.
3. Cú Chulainn was trained by Scáthach, a renowned warrior woman in Scotland. She honed his fighting skills and taught him how to use his magic spear, Gáe Bulg.
4. Some of Cú Chulainn's superhuman gifts included magic, poetry, warfare, and wisdom. He also had a transformation called riastrad, where he transformed into an undefeatable supernatural monster.
5. Cú Chulainn was tricked into breaking his taboos by his enemies, which weakened him and made him vulnerable. He was served dog meat by an old woman. This led to his defeat in a battle against Lugaid mac Con Roí, who hated Cú Chulainn for having an affair with his mother and killing his father. Cú Chulainn was wounded and tied himself to a standing stone, where he died from his wounds. He was beheaded by Lugaid after his death.

Chapter 5: The Flame of Saint Brigid

Brigid (*brih-jid*) was a daughter of the Dagda, the father figure and chief deity in the mythical race of the Tuatha Dé Danann. Her mother is said to be Danu, the ancient mother goddess from whom the Tuatha Dé Danann sprang. Like all the other deities of this race, Brigid was the goddess of multiple things.

Her benevolence and association with many joyous occasions like spring, dawn, and renewal made her one of the most popular gods in Ireland. In fact, sagas in which Brigid is mentioned sometimes appear to make her the patron of anything and everything that a follower could wish her to be. She was a personal deity to many Irish people. She protected the vulnerable, women, children, plants, and animals.

Some scholars are of the opinion that Brigid is actually a triple goddess—three sisters that function together. There are several examples of this phenomenon in Irish mythology. They suggest that Brigid was the goddess of spring and that her sisters were goddesses of health and smithing.

Springtime Is Brigid's Time!

Brigid appeared in different forms, representing aspects of strength, renewal, fertility, and wisdom. Most agree that she was just one goddess, but many also believe that she was a shapeshifter. She always appeared as a woman, but she could be young and beautiful, motherly and middle-aged, or a wise old woman. She took whatever form was needed for the situation.

Goddess of Fire

Brigid's original domain as the goddess of fire naturally linked her to the warm and cozy environment of the home. The sunlight and warmth of the spring season linked her to seasonal cycles, planting, growth, and harvests. This linked her to the fertility of humans, animals, and plants. She symbolized renewal and transformation.

In this role, she was depicted as a red-haired, beautiful, young maiden. Some myths even have her dressed in sunlight, her flowing hair sparkling with flames. Her main festival, known as Imbolc, is a celebration halfway between the winter and summer equinoxes. Imbolc was celebrated with large bonfires and great feasts.

Brigid's Flame

The Celts made a fire in honor of Brigid that burned perpetually at a shrine for her in Kildare, Ireland. According to this legend, a group of nineteen flame keepers kept this flame burning for many centuries. Some say they were priestesses of the Druids. They were also called *inghean an Dagha* (*in-yen un dah-ga*), meaning daughters of the fire.

Saint Brigid of Kildare.[14]

After the Christian monks came to Ireland, several attempts were made to extinguish this fire, but these seemed to have been unsuccessful. In the 12th century, a Welsh chronicler wrote that Brigid's flame was still burning. It was tended by a group of Catholic nuns.

This is most likely because the ancient pagan goddess Brigid was Christianized by Saint Patrick. Her pagan legacy was no longer a threat to Christianity. Christians could view the perpetual flame as the new light that Christianity brought to Ireland.

We do not know when Brigid's flame was extinguished. It was relit in 1993 by the Mother Superior of the Brigidine Sisters of Kildare. In neopaganism and some Wiccan circles, followers also keep a flame burning, and rituals include tending this flame by a selected group.

In 2005, the local council of Kildare erected a statue for Saint Brigid's flame in their town square. The statue has a twisted trunk with large oak leaves at the top. A bronze acorn on top of the oak's leaves carries the flame, which is still tended by the Brigidine nuns today. It symbolizes the wish for hope, justice, and peace.

Muse of Poets

Brigid was a patron of the arts, which made her a beloved goddess among bards, poets, and songwriters. She inspired and encouraged their use of words to describe feelings that reverberate in the hearts of listeners and readers alike. Songs and the oral transmission of stories and histories were sacred to the ancient Celts.

Goddess of Healing

Intertwined with Brigid's roles as a fertility goddess and goddess of spring were her roles in protection and healing. She was revered as an agricultural and livestock goddess who could ensure the safety and fertility of their animals and crops. Wells were named after Brigid since believers thought the water had healing powers.

Christianization of the Myths of Brigid

Various Catholic monks tried to convert the Irish to Christianity. It proved a bit difficult since their pagan religion was very old and well embedded in their culture. Saint Patrick, the monk who is credited with bringing Christianity to Ireland, learned that it was easier to build Christian beliefs, saints, and festivals into the already existing beliefs. In the case of Brigid, all he needed to do was recognize a pious young woman with a pure heart as a saintly person who could replace the ancient goddess Brigid in the hearts of the people. This Brigid was posthumously recognized as a saint through tradition rather than canonization. She is credited, along with Saint Patrick, for spreading Christianity through Ireland. Over time, her many good deeds were intertwined with the myths of the pagan goddess Brigid.

Stained glass image of Saint Brigid.[15]

Brigid, with all her qualities of gentleness, kindness, and good deeds, fits nicely into this adaptable category of changing pagan myths into Christian miracles. And so, the new Christian Brigid became a saint with whom some of the old goddess Brigid's traditions and special places could be associated! There are even tales that she was revered by some as a foster mother of Jesus Christ. Others say that she was the midwife who tended Mary during the birth of Jesus. In addition, pagan Brigid was already honored by a cross made from rushes, which could be easily adapted to symbolize the holy cross of Christianity.

The Story of Saint Brigid

Medieval literature says that the Christian Saint Brigid was born around 451 CE in Kildare. Today, she is one of the three patron saints of Ireland. Folktales tell us that she was born at the entrance of the house of a Druid. Her father was a nobleman, and her mother was a slave. Sunlight formed a bright halo around her head at her birth.

When Brigid was a child, the house where she lived caught fire. It was considered a miracle when the flames did not destroy the house. Brigid was not hurt in any way. When beggars and a hungry dog came to the house, Brigid gave them food. She miraculously managed to replace the food so her own family did not go hungry.

She became a housemaid for her father's family when she was older. It was said that the food never ran out when Brigid did the cooking. She was kind and generous. She displayed many of the characteristics once ascribed to the goddess Brigid. She ran away to Saint Patrick when she learned that her father had arranged a marriage for her. By that point, she had already decided to spend her life in the service of Christ.

A close friendship developed between Brigid and Saint Patrick. It was recorded in the *Book of Armagh* (ar-mah), a 9th-century illuminated manuscript of the life of Saint Patrick. The scribe wrote that they were perfectly in tune with each other's views on the role of charity in Christianity. Saint Brigid is even buried next to Saint Patrick at Downpatrick.

In 468 CE, Brigid and seven other pious women formed the first female monastic community in Ireland. They helped the poor and provided them with food that appeared to never run out. Her many miracles included a well with healing waters that she made to suddenly appear from the ground.

A blind nun was once given the gift of sight by Saint Brigid. When the nun saw the wickedness going on around her, she asked Brigid to return her blindness. She told Brigid that the sight of the eyes blinded the sight from the soul.

Saint Brigid's most famous miracle was when she went to ask the king of Leinster for a piece of ground on which to build a monastery. The spiteful king said she could have as much land as her cloak could cover. Miraculously, Brigid's cloak kept spreading until it covered enough ground for a large monastery and all its outbuildings!

Saint Brigid and nine of her companions built the monastery in the latter half of the 5th century CE under an oak tree. It is said that it was on the same site where the old shrine of the goddess Brigid stood. They also incorporated the goddess Brigid's flame. It became the Flame of Saint Brigid, and a group of nuns tended it.

The monastery developed into a large complex that included both a cloister for nuns and a monastery for monks. The position of the abbess always remained superior to that of the abbot. Buildings for arts and crafts, including metalwork, were added. It soon became a center of learning for scholars and artisans. They produced manuscripts, poetry, artwork, and metalworks.

Chapter 5 Activity

Can you answer the questions below?

1. What are some of the domains that Brigid was the goddess of?
_____
_____
_____
_____

2. What is Brigid's Flame, and how was it maintained?
_____
_____
_____
_____

3. What roles did Brigid play in healing and protection?
_____
_____
_____
_____

4. Who was responsible for the Christianization of Brigid?
_____
_____
_____
_____

5. What are some of the stories about Saint Brigid's life and miracles?
_____
_____
_____
_____

Answers

1. Brigid was the goddess of a multitude of domains. She was associated with many joyous occasions like spring, dawn, and renewal. She protected the vulnerable, women, children, plants, and animals.

2. Brigid's flame was a fire made in honor of Brigid. It burned perpetually at a shrine for her in Kildare, Ireland. It was maintained by a group of nineteen flame keepers who kept this flame burning for many centuries.

3. Brigid was revered as an agricultural and livestock goddess who could ensure the safety and fertility of animals and crops. Wells were named after Brigid. Believers thought that the water had healing powers.

4. The ancient pagan goddess Brigid was Christianized by Saint Patrick as Saint Brigid.

5. When Saint Brigid was a child, the house where she lived caught fire. The flames did not destroy the house, and Brigid was not hurt in any way. Brigid helped the poor and provided them with food that never appeared to run out. Her other miracles included a well with healing waters, which she made to suddenly appear from the ground.

Chapter 6: The Morrigan's Shadow

The Morrigan is the phantom queen of Irish mythology. Do not be confused by the definite article usually accompanying her name. She is often referred to as "the "Morrigan because neither her ancient followers nor the later scribes could decide whether she was one being or a triple goddess (a group of three sisters working together). Frankly, neither can we!

An Overview of the Morrigan

During the time when the Tuatha Dé Danann ruled Ireland, Morrigan was the wife of the Dagda. She was a jealous queen. Who could blame her? The Dagda was known for his many wives and affairs. She could also be spiteful in her revenge against the women the Dagda became involved with. In one account, she takes away a woman's prize breeding bull to the Otherworld, thus robbing her of her income.

This brave woman, who might have been involved with the Dagda, followed Morrigan into a cave that led to the Otherworld. There, the woman fell asleep, and Morrigan turned her into a spring that made a pool of water that drained into the River Shannon.

Like Brigid, the Morrigan is sometimes portrayed as a triple goddess or three sisters, each representing an aspect of her main domain. Unlike Brigid, the Morrigan was associated with death, fate, doom, war, and **sovereignty** (*rule* or *power*). Strangely, the Morrigan was also seen as a guardian of the land, its animals, and its people. In this guise, she played the role of protector when Ireland was threatened.

She actively participated in battles to encourage Ireland's warriors and sow fear amongst their enemies. She often flew as a black crow over the battlefield and selected who would be victorious and who would die.

The Morrigan as a crow in a 1911 illustration.[16]

The Morrigan was a shapeshifter. She could appear as a beautiful young woman or an old crone. She even appears as a raven, a black crow, or other animals on occasion. During one battle, she appeared to the great Irish hero, Cú Chulainn, in five different forms in one day! She was the most active during the mythological cycle of the Tuatha Dé Danann and in the Ulster Cycle of Irish mythology. However, she is very much a part of today's pagan beliefs.

Speculations on the Origin of the Morrigan

For linguists, the answer lies in the interpretation of the Morrigan's name. Linking her to the Arthurian tales of Morgan le Fay is out, mainly because the root "mor" means "sea." For other scholars, the triple-goddess theory is only plausible because it is a well-established phenomenon in ancient Celtic mythology. According to the triple-goddess theory, the three sisters are Badb (*bive*), Macha (*mah-kha*), and Nemain (*neh-vin*).

She was the wife of the Dagda in old oral histories. She was also the granddaughter of King Nuada of the Tuatha Dé Danann in other myths. The Dagda and Nuada were brothers and the sons of the mother goddess Danu, though. This is an example of the complexity of many mythological tales.

According to ancient myths from the 1st century CE, the Morrigan, in the form of the three sisters, was worshiped by the cult of the mothers. The roots of this cult were thought to date back to the Stone Age. As Macha, the Morrigan was a fierce protector of the land and its freedom. She was the goddess of sovereignty. As Badb, she was the enforcer of death, battles, and war. As Nemain, she brought bloodshed and fury to the battlefield.

In written sources, the oldest mention of the Morrigan dates to *The Cattle Raid of Cooley* in the Ulster Cycle. The Ulster Cycle was after the Tuatha Dé Danann had been driven to the Otherworld by the Milesians. The Morrigan would have been a spiritual being of the Sidhe and not a part of the Tuatha Dé Danann while they were the rulers of Ireland. But we are talking about mythology here, so anything is possible!

Folktales and Myths of the Morrigan

The Morrigan predicted a warrior's death by appearing to them as an old woman washing their bloody battle clothes. On the battlefield, she took on the form of a crow. It was said that the crow's actions would stir fear in the hearts of the enemy while generating courage and fervor in the side she favored. Let us have a look at her involvement in some of the major battles in Ireland.

The Second Battle of Mag Tuired

The Morrigan had a romantic encounter with the Dagda before this battle against the Fomorians. She promised him that the Fomorians would be defeated forever in the coming battle. It is said that the Morrigan magically caused fire and blood to rain down on the Fomorians before the fighting began.

Some sources say that she promised Dagda that she would call the demons of the air to put a spell on the Fomorians. She also promised to kill the Fomorian king and take his blood and kidneys—sources of his strength and courage. She promised to deposit these items in the river where she and the Dagda met.

The spell sowed fear and confusion even in the hearts of the Fomorians. This led to an easy victory for the Tuatha Dé Danann. In one version of this tale, the Fomorians were driven back into the sea.

The Morrigan cursing the men of Ulster.[17]

Encounters with Cú Chulainn

Cú Chulainn's first encounter with the Morrigan was during the Cattle Raid of Cooley. His battles with each of Queen Medb's champions took place at different fords of a river. He killed them one by one. Between these battles, the Morrigan appeared to him as a beautiful woman. She even tried to seduce him.

As a disciplined warrior, Cú Chulainn did not allow himself to be distracted from his cause. He refused to fall for her charm. The Morrigan was offended. She turned into a raven and sat on a branch. Cú Chulainn instantly recognized her as the goddess. The ancient Irish people were wary of a vision of the Morrigan since her appearance usually meant someone would die.

Cú Chulainn with the Morrigan as a black crow above him predicting his death.[18]

Cú Chulainn told her that he would have acted differently if he had known it was her, but it was too late. She was already offended. He had made an enemy of her. The Morrigan predicted his death in a future battle and that she would be there for it.

When Cú Chulainn resumed his battles with Queen Medb's champions, the Morrigan hindered his progress. She appeared as an eel that tried to trip him, and he had to kill it. Next, she appeared as a wolf and tried to cause a stampede with the brown bull. Cú Chulainn killed the wolf and stopped the stampede. Finally, she appeared as a white heifer with red ears that led the herd to stampede. Again, Cú Chulainn had no choice but to wound the animal.

After the battle, the Morrigan appeared to Cú Chulainn as a wounded old woman leading a cow. She offered the thirsty warrior some milk. He did not recognize her, but he was puzzled that her wounds were in exactly the same places where he had struck the three animals that bothered him during his fights against Medb's champions.

Despite his suspicion, he accepted three drinks of milk from her. After every drink, he thanked her with a blessing, and after each blessing, one of the woman's wounds miraculously healed. Cú Chulainn knew then that it was the Morrigan. She predicted that there was great bloodshed still to come and that she would be there at his death. In his final battle, the dying Cú Chulainn, who had sworn to die on his feet, lashed himself to a standing stone. With his last breath, he beckoned his enemies to attack. They were confused that he was still standing and hesitated. It was only when the Morrigan in her black crow guise perched on his shoulder that they realized his end had arrived.

The Morrigan in Modern Cultures

In neopaganism and neo-Druidism, the Morrigan's vast powers over sovereignty, life, death, and fate are an inspiration to their followers. It inspires people, especially women, to strive for independence and transformation with strength and resilience. Ceremonies for the Morrigan include rituals to gain her cooperation for personal change and growth.

In Wicca (modern witchcraft), the Morrigan is revered as a triple goddess, something which neopaganism and neo-Druidism deny. However, these religions follow most of the same beliefs.

A difference between ancient and modern Morrigan followers appears to be in the symbols representing her. In ancient times, the main symbol of the Morrigan was a black crow (sometimes mistaken for a raven). Today, a crow, a raven, a version of the triquetra (Celtic trinity knot), and other Celtic symbols are seen as symbols of the Morrigan. A **triquetra** (*try-kwet-ra*) is an intricate series of twists and turns of lines or strings with no discernible beginning or end.

To sum up, the Morrigan's role in modern paganism is as a powerful protector and inspirer of women and children. She helps by teaching her followers to embrace their inner strength to accomplish difficult changes and improve themselves. Through the Morrigan's inspiration for action, modern pagans are often involved in activism for positive change.

Chapter 6 Activity

Answer the following questions.

1. Who is the Morrigan in Irish mythology, and why is she often referred to as "the" Morrigan?

2. Who was the Morrigan's husband? How is she depicted in her relationship with him?

3. How is the Morrigan involved in battles? What form does she often take on the battlefield?

4. What happened in the Second Battle of Mag Tuired, and what role did the Morrigan play in it?

5. How is the Morrigan depicted in modern cultures, such as neopaganism and neo-Druidism?

Answers

1. The Morrigan is the phantom queen of Irish mythology. She is often referred to as "the" Morrigan because neither her ancient followers nor the later scribes could decide whether she was one being or a triple goddess (a group of three sisters working together).

2. During the time when the Tuatha Dé Danann ruled Ireland, the Morrigan was the wife of the Dagda. She was a jealous queen and was known for her spiteful revenge.

3. The Morrigan actively participated in battles to encourage Ireland's warriors and sow chaos amongst their enemies. She often flew as a black crow over the battlefield and selected who would be victorious and who would die.

4. In the Second Battle of Mag Tuired, the Morrigan had a romantic encounter with the Dagda before the battle. She promised him that the Fomorians would be defeated in the coming battle.

5. In neopaganism and neo-Druidism, Morrigan's vast powers over sovereignty, life, death, and fate are an inspiration to followers. It inspires people, especially women, to strive for independence and to deal with changes with strength and resilience.

Chapter 7: Druids and Magic

Like the Tuatha Dé Danann, the Druids and their practices were mysterious. Irish folktales tell us that the secretive Druids were forbidden to write down their knowledge, crafts, and magic skills. Scholars still debate whether they were a separate clan or whether they were selected from the different clans of Ireland to be trained as Druids.

The Druids were present all across western Europe, including Britain and Ireland, during the Bronze and Iron Ages. Some scholars believe they can connect ancient relics and paintings from caves dating back thousands of years in Europe to ancient mystics who later became the Druids. They trace the earliest practices of the known Druids to the mysticism reflected in these cave paintings. This remains a highly debatable theory, as it cannot be proved. There is also no certainty about when the Druids first appeared among the Celtic tribes or when they first entered Ireland.

The origin of the Druids, their knowledge, and their secret practices have allowed wild, weird, and wonderful stories to develop around them. If you are a science-fiction and fantasy fan, allow your imagination to fly! Were the Druids magicians or healers with extraordinary powers and secret knowledge? Were they relics of a lost, advanced ancient civilization that infiltrated newly settled hunter-gatherer tribes?

The Druids did not have temples or churches. They worshiped in nature, often in groves of oaks and forests. They believed that the oak and the hazelnut were the most sacred trees. Groves and forests provided them with cover for secret rituals and the training of new recruits. It is possible that some of the Druid elders and sages lived in the forests and groves on a permanent basis.

The Druids as Described by Outsiders

The Druids' role verges between history and mythology. The Romans wrote about their powerful influence and control over the people. Several Catholic monks wrote about their roles, acts, and influence. They recorded that the Druids were the priests, healers, historians, judges, and magicians of the Celts.

It was recorded by observers that the Druids were so powerful amongst their people that a single Druid could stop a battle between tribes by merely jumping in between the two armies.

A Druid in his role as a judge.[19]

The Druids and Oral History

For the Celts, the Druids were sages, bards, prophets, diviners, poets, educators, judges, and the protectors of all spiritual and earthly knowledge. When oral history was recorded by Christian scribes, they emphasized the complex nature of the Druids' influence. They were the chief counselors of the kings of Ireland. As spiritual leaders, they were the priests responsible for the religious rituals and practices of the Celtic tribes. They were responsible for sacrifices in honor of the deities.

The bards were a class of Druids who moved among the clans. They were the storytellers who sang and recited the ancient stories of the tribes. The **ovates** (*oh-vayts*) were another class of Druids. They were the healers, diviners, and seers. Each class of Druids had multiple roles regarding the moral and spiritual health and knowledge of the tribes.

Druids could be male or female. Female Druids were referred to as Bandruí (*bahn-dree*). Druids could get married and have children. The Dagda of the Tuatha Dé Danann was said to have been a Druid and a deity.

Roman Times: Annihilation and Bloodshed

The Romans who invaded Britain hated the Druids for their influence over the people. They were driven to the western reaches of the island. The Druids made a stand on the island of Anglesey off the coast of Wales. They were all slaughtered in a bloody battle by the Romans. All their considerable knowledge was lost to history.

The Romans never succeeded in conquering Ireland. There, the Druids' knowledge and skills even survived Christianization. In medieval writings, some of the knowledge that had been orally transmitted from generation to generation was recorded. It was translated from Latin and Old Irish by scholars around the 17th century.

Ancient Megalithic Monuments

Some modern traditions of Druidic followers connect the Druids to the stone monuments of Ireland and Britain. They believe that the construction of the ancient mounds and tombs like Newgrange was planned and overseen by Druids. The astronomical, mathematical, and engineering knowledge ascribed to the Druids, coupled with their spiritual teachings, fit well with this hypothesis of whether Druids were really in Ireland long before the Celts.

The earliest Irish manmade wonder dates back to between 6400 and 4600 BCE. This makes them older than the pyramids of Egypt and the well-known Stonehenge in England. There are signs that the sites were used, although not for their original purposes, well into the Common Era. Chances are good that they were used as gathering places for celebrations of ancient festivals well into Christian times.

Training of the Druids

Young people from across Ireland were often sent to spend time with the Druids to be educated. Of course, this education was not the same education that those training to become Druids received. The education of the youth was focused on moral and religious behavior in society. This included lessons on the laws of the land, basic mathematics, chivalry, and the treatment of others and the environment.

Young Druids were taught in-depth knowledge, and they had to learn to recite their knowledge by heart. They served an apprenticeship of up to twenty years. We do not know whether each Druid learned all of the Druids' knowledge. That would have been a massive task since it included mathematics, astronomy, astrology, divination, natural sciences, history, social sciences, laws, and more.

It is speculated that they were taught the basics of all Druid knowledge and then specialized in certain areas. One can probably compare it to choosing your field of study when going to college or university.

There were also those who became Druid sages—the keepers of the most sacred knowledge of mysticism and magic. This sacred knowledge was kept secret, so it was lost over time. It is speculated that initiates underwent a form of spiritual rebirth before being allowed into the inner circle of sacred knowledge.

This spiritual rebirth might have included periods of sensory deprivation. Initiates would experience a lengthy period of isolation, fasting, and meditating in a dark cave or in tombs with no light or human contact. They would experience the moment of rejoining their community in the light as a rebirth.

Belief System of the Druids

The ancient Druids were polytheistic. They believed in many gods, mostly those connected to aspects of the natural world. The Druids honored all of nature, especially trees, rivers, and rocks.

They also believed that the present was tied to the past in the form of ancestor veneration. They believed that the spirits of their ancestors had an influence over their family in the present. Ancestors could advise and steer circumstances in favor of their descendants. Druids also believed in the immortality of the soul and its reincarnation in certain instances.

The Druids believed that everything in the cosmos was interrelated in a spiritual realm. To the Druids, death was a natural part of the cycle of life. They saw communication with the spiritual Otherworld as a normal interaction that kept harmony and balance. We can say that a true Druid saw the world and everything in it from a spiritual viewpoint.

Death and Dying

The Druids taught that the soul or spirit of a person resided in the head. They believed that death was merely a time of transition from one realm to the other between the material world and the Otherworld. They also believed in reincarnation because the spirit had to progress through more than one life in order to become fully versed in the three ultimate goals of wisdom, creativity, and enduring love for all of creation. Some believed that their reincarnation could be in different forms, such as animals and plants.

In Irish folk tradition, after someone died—particularly after a funeral—people often kept their distance from the sick, believing that fairy spirits might be nearby to claim another soul. Homes were kept warm, and bright fires were maintained to keep such spirits at bay. It was customary to open windows and doors after a death so that the soul could leave without being trapped.

After Christianization, a Christian monk rather than a Druid would be seen by the bedside of someone who was dying. It was believed that the best time to die was the twelve days of Christmas since the gates of heaven stayed open for both the righteous and sinners during this time.

Ceremonies and Rituals

The power of the Druids was so great that they were called upon to choose a king. They did this by performing a ritual and entering a trancelike state that led them to select the right person.

The Druids were seen as the connection between the natural and supernatural worlds. They decided on feast days and how celebrations would be held to honor the deities and seasonal changes. The Druids called on the deities and made sacrifices in times of war and disasters. They also oversaw rites of passage like births, marriages, deaths, and funerals.

Druids inciting the Britons to oppose the Romans.[20]

The Druids would lead the people of Ireland in worship and **supplication** (*appeal*) to certain deities in times of need. The ancient Roman writers, including Julius Caesar, recorded gruesome accounts of human sacrifice.

One description told of how a person was enclosed in a wicker cage that was hung on an oak tree. The cage was set on fire, and the person inside slowly burned to death. We must bear in mind that the account was written by the Druids' enemy. They wanted to paint the Druids as cruel barbarians. It is a bit strange that the Druids would endanger a tree by burning somebody hanging from that tree!

Magic Skills of the Druids

The Druids were seen as diviners and seers who could interpret omens and predict the future. They were thought to be able to control elements of nature like the wind and storms. They were supposed to have the power to become invisible or shapeshift when necessary. They were more like sorcerers rather than shamans to outsiders.

Their walking sticks were seen as magic wands by the Irish. For instance, they could put a person or group into an unnatural sleep with their walking sticks.

Tales of the Druids

It is sometimes fascinating to note how similar mythologies of different ancient peoples of the world can be. In the case of Ireland and Greece, there are several similarities. The myth of Cian (*kee-an*) and Eithne (*eth-nya*) in Ireland is a lot like the story of Danae and Zeus in Greek mythology.

The Story of Eithne and Cian

Eithne was the beautiful daughter of Balor. He was a cruel one-eyed giant who was one of the kings of the Fomorians in the time of the Tuatha Dé Danann. Balor was also known as Balor of the Evil Eye. Anyone who looked into his single eye would die instantly. A prophet told Balor that he would be killed by his own grandson.

When Eithne was growing up, Balor locked her in a tower to prevent her from ever meeting a man and having a child. Eithne had a recurring dream in which she saw the face of a handsome young man. This face belonged to Cian, a king of the Tuatha Dé Danann. Eithne longed to meet him. At night, Eithne would sit on the roof of her tower and stare out at the sea, longing for this man whom she had never met.

With the help of a Bandruí (a female Druid) named Birog (*bir-ug*), Cian eventually met Eithne. Birog's magic wind carried her and Cian to the tower of Eithne. Of course, it was love at first sight! Unfortunately, Birog's magic did not stretch far enough to set Eithne free, so after a while, she had to fly back with Cian to his throne.

Poor Eithne was heartbroken, but her sadness turned to joy when she found out she was pregnant. When her baby was born, the furious Balor took the baby from Eithne and threw him into the sea. All the people watching thought the baby boy was dead.

Meanwhile, Birog had been watching carefully. As soon as the baby sank under the waves, she grabbed him and flew with him to his father. Cian was overjoyed and showered his son with love and everything he could ever want. He named him Lugh.

When the boy was a young man, he became the leader of the army of the Tuatha Dé Danann in the Second Battle of Mag Tuired. Balor was one of the leaders of the Fomorian forces in this battle. Lugh killed Balor in this battle by shooting his evil eye out with a slingshot. The eye was blasted right through Balor's head and out through the back. Balor's eye was struck with such force that it flew into the midst of Balor's own warriors, who died on the spot after looking at it. In another version, Lugh used a magic "scorching" stone in his slingshot. However it happened, the prophecy was fulfilled!

This is yet another example of two different stories about the same character. Remember Lugh, who came with the Tuatha Dé Danann and owned the magic spear that gave him the nickname Lugh of the Long Arm? In this story, he is born in Ireland, with his parents being a Fomorian princess and his father a mortal human.

The Legend of Tlachtga

Tales were told of the mightiest Bandruí to tread the soil of Ireland. Her name was Tlachtga (*cloch-ga*). She was the daughter of a blind Druid prince in County Kerry. It was said that she was fearless, wild, and strong. She was also beautiful and intelligent. She learned all the knowledge of the Irish Druids from her father, but it did not satisfy her curiosity.

Her father taught her the Druids' magic of divination and how to have power over the weather, such as raising a storm with her breath. She watched and studied everything around her until she figured out how everything worked in nature. Then, when her father was a very old man, she took him with her from the shores of **Eire** (Ireland) to travel the world and learn about other people, their knowledge, their secrets, and their lands.

Tlachtga made a magic-wheeled vehicle from the sacred rowan trees. It was drawn by two oxen and could fly through the sky. Its sides were made of glass, which shimmered so brightly that it could blind a person who looked directly at it.

Their trip was interrupted in Jerusalem, where they met Simon Magus. Their divining had shown them that something great was soon to be revealed there. Tlachtga left her father there and went on alone to the four great cities of the mysterious north, where the sages had taught the Tuatha Dé Danann.

When Tlachtga returned to Jerusalem, she knew more than her father and Simon Magus together. Simon was jealous and conspired with his three sons to assault her. The legend does not explain why she was not able to stop them with her powerful magic, but she became pregnant as a result. After that, she returned to County Meath in Ireland and died giving birth to three sons fathered by the cold-hearted sons of Simon Magus.

She named three nearby plains after her three sons. Before she died, she prophesied that no harm would come to Ireland as long as those plains were kept sacred. The future kings of Meath were all descendants of her three sons.

Over time, the prophecy was forgotten, customs changed, and harm came to Ireland. Then, the people remembered, and the Druids made special fires at Samhain to honor all the deities because the rites requested by Tlachtga had been forgotten. When Ireland was Christianized, this festival became All Saints' Day.

Modern Revival of Druid Legacy

There are many groups of modern Druids across the world. Some are even online! Some people study and follow Druidic practices without being Druids. In Ireland, modern Druidism is a blend of reviving the old traditions with modern adaptations. The reality is that interpretations of ancient practices vary greatly because all that lost oral knowledge can never be recovered. The ancient Druids' secret knowledge and magic practices were never written down and never disclosed to outsiders, even by Druids who became Christians.

Modern interpretations of ancient Druidic beliefs are based on folktales and observations by hostile third parties. Very little is known directly from ancient Druid teachings due to the lack of records. The goals of neo-Druidism circles include reforging a lost bond between spirituality and nature. Elements of protecting, nourishing, and healing the environment play a major role in neo-Druidism.

Despite a period of romanticizing the mysticism of the Druids in recent centuries, today's Druidic circles include scholars. Their research and study of the subject matter are admired even in academic circles. Like the rest of Ireland's mythology, Druids are also characters in modern novels, movies, video games, and comic books.

Modern Druids celebrating the solstice at Stonehenge.[21]

The Druids participate in modern Celtic seasonal festivals such as Lughnasadh (*loo-nuh-suh*) (start of the harvest), Samhain (*sah-win*) (modern-day Halloween), Imbolc (start of spring), and Beltane (*bel-tun*) (beginning of summer). They have eight official festivals, including the solstices and the equinoxes. Many unofficial celebrations and memorable occasions are celebrated by neo-Druid circles. The festivities are usually accompanied by chanting, music, singing, and poetry readings.

Chapter 7 Activity

Can you answer the following questions? If you have trouble coming up with the answers, make sure to reread the chapter.

1. Who were the Druids? What kind of roles did they play in Celtic society?

_____
_____
_____
_____

2. How did the Druids worship, and what did they believe were the most sacred trees?

_____
_____
_____
_____

3. What happened to the Druids during the Roman invasion of Britain?

_____
_____
_____
_____

4. How were young Druids trained? What did their education include?

_____
_____
_____
_____

Answers

1. The Druids were a mysterious group in Irish mythology. They were forbidden to write down their knowledge. Scholars still debate whether they were a separate clan or whether they were selected from the different clans of Ireland to be trained as Druids. The Druids were the priests, healers, historians, judges, and magicians of the Celts.

2. The Druids did not have temples or churches. They worshiped in nature, often in groves of oaks and forests, because of their closeness to nature. They believed that the oak and hazelnut were the most sacred trees.

3. The Romans who invaded Britain hated the Druids for their influence over the people. They were driven to the western reaches of the country. They made a stand on the island of Anglesey off the coast of Wales. They were slaughtered in a bloody battle by the Romans.

4. Young Druids were taught in-depth knowledge, and they had to learn to recite their knowledge by heart. They served an apprenticeship of up to twenty years. Their education included mathematics, astronomy, astrology, divination, natural sciences, history, social sciences, laws, and more.

Chapter 8: The Fenian Cycle

Let us take a closer look at the Fenian Cycle, the era of the Fianna that we looked at earlier. This cycle of Irish mythology falls between the Ulster Cycle and the Kings' Cycle. The Fenian Cycle's tales, poems, ballads, and history were recorded in several manuscripts between 600 and 1400 CE.

We ended the tales of the Fianna where they were annihilated by the king's army. In this version, only Oisín, Fionn mac Cumhaill's son, and Caoilte remained. They traveled throughout Ireland as poets and storytellers, just like the bards, and related their stories to the people they came across.

Many of the tales of the Fenian Cycle involve Ireland and Scotland, with each claiming ownership of some of the heroes and deeds. James McGregor, the dean (a cleric) of Lismore, and his brother wrote a Scottish manuscript called the *Book of the Dean of Lismore* in Gaelic, in which many tales of the Fianna are included. The content was published as translations of ancient Gaelic manuscripts. However, it was proved by the 19th century that much of it was McGregor's own romanticized fiction.

The Book of Lismore

Page from the 1890 Book of Lismore.[22]

In the late 15th century, the Book of Lismore, or the Book of Mac Carthaig Riabhach (*mac kawr-hee ree-uh-vakh*), was written in Irish for Lord Carbery, Finghean Mac Carthaigh (*fin-yen mac kawr-hee*) of County Cork, Ireland. About a quarter of the manuscript survived, and it covers the deeds and legends of the Fianna and Fionn Mac Cumhaill.

The manuscript also contains Irish history, poetry, prose, and stories from European sources, such as Marco Polo's adventures. About half of the surviving manuscript is dedicated to stories of Catholic saints, combining Irish legends and history. This shows how ancient Celtic beliefs were blended into Christian stories to make them more acceptable to the Irish.

The Dialogue of The Old Men

Oisín had a companion named Caoilte, who returned from Tír na nÓg with him. They found that three hundred years had passed in their absence. They immediately turned into two very old men, but they somehow stayed alive. Saint Patrick, the patron saint of Ireland, was there when they returned. Saint Patrick summoned them, and they told him all their stories of Ireland's ancient heroes. Saint Patrick ordered his scribe to record their account. It was later compiled in The Dialogue of the Old Men around the 12th century.

The aged Oisín tells Saint Patrick the stories of the Fianna.[28]

After Oisín died, Caoilte traveled with Saint Patrick, telling him the history and lore of each place they visited.

Legend of the Giant's Causeway

Fionn mac Cumhaill was a giant in this legend. He had to defend Ireland against a giant named Benandonner (*ben-un-don-er*), who came from Scotland. Benandonner planned to invade and take over the beautiful Emerald Isle for himself. Fionn was livid. He started throwing rocks into the sea.

He saw that his rocks had created a perfect road stretching into the sea. Fionn suddenly had an epiphany (*moment of inspiration*). If he threw enough rocks in the same manner, he could build a causeway connecting him to Scotland. He could challenge Benandonner in person to decide the fate of Ireland.

After sneaking onto the Scottish isle of Staffa via his new bridge, he saw Benandonner for the first time. He was shocked to discover that the Scottish giant was much larger than he was! Fionn had to change his plans because Benandonner would probably beat him in a duel. He had to outwit him with a cunning plan instead.

The Giant's Causeway.[24]

The resourceful Fionn mac Cumhaill talked his wife into disguising him as a baby. Just as Fionn had planned, Benandonner saw the causeway. He decided to cross into Ireland right then and there to finish off their protector and champion so he could forcibly take the land. He got the fright of his life when he found Fionn's home and saw a woman tending to her enormous baby. If that was Fionn's baby, Fionn must be huge! Benandonner became scared at the thought of such a giant and decided to flee.

As he fled across the causeway, he began picking up the rocks behind him, breaking up the bridge. He threw them as far as he could into the sea so that Fionn would never be able to rebuild the bridge. The start of this causeway is still there today.

The Legend of Cath Loduinn From Oisín's Ballads

The hero of this Ossian ballad is Fingal or Fionnghall, which means "white stranger" in Gaelic. Fingal sets out on a voyage to the Scottish Orkney Islands, but his ship is driven to Scandinavia by a storm. He lands in the kingdom of Starno, a cruel Scandinavian king. The king invites Fingal to a feast, but he refuses since he knows about this king's reputation. Fingal prepares to defend himself while Starno gathers his people.

Fingal roams around the area during the night. He meets a beautiful maiden from a neighboring kingdom whom Starno kept locked in a cave. He also finds a shrine where Starno and his son consulted a spirit about a coming war. Unfortunately, the translations of the poem do not conclude the main story. How did the battle end? Did Fingal set the maiden of the cave free?

In the same ballad, two brothers fight over the king's daughter. It is not clear whether this is King Starno's prisoner (the princess in the cave) or his own daughter. One brother is killed, and the other is exiled by their father. He ends up living in a land far away. However, he is not alone. By his side is the beautiful princess.

In another version of the ballad, King Starno kills his daughter or the princess locked in the cave. He sees her as a traitor because she warned Fingal that she had overheard the king and his son discussing a plot to kill him.

The Pursuit of Diarmuid and Grainne

Diarmuid Ua Duibhne (*deer-mid oo-a div-nya*) was one of the Fianna. He was a brave and loyal hero. He was also the friend of their leader, Fionn mac Cumhaill. The handsome young man had a reputation for attracting women. This was due to a magic love spot bestowed on him by a beautiful young sorceress.

Grainne (*grawn-ya*) was the feisty and gorgeous daughter of King Cormac mac Airt (*art*), the high king of Ireland who created the Fianna. Grainne was promised to Fionn as his bride, even though he was quite a bit older than her. She was not in love with Fionn and was unhappy with this arrangement.

At the betrothal feast of Fionn and Grainne, she fell madly in love with Diarmuid. The bold and charming young woman made a plan. She moved among the guests, chatting and laughing with everyone. Meanwhile, she was casting a sleeping spell on them. In some retellings, she was sneaking a drug into their drinks. As they all lay sleeping, Grainne put a binding spell on Diarmuid, compelling him to run away with her.

When the guests and Fionn woke up, they realized the two were missing. At first, they thought the pair had been abducted. Soon, however, Fionn realized

An illustration of Grainne.[25]

they had run away together. He was furious, thinking they had been having an affair behind his back. He and his loyal band of Fianna chased them across Ireland.

Diarmuid was torn between Grainne and his loyalty to Fionn and the Fianna, but he fell deeply in love with Grainne while they were on the run. After many years in hiding, they were tired. Grainne was pregnant. It was cold and snowing, and they knew they had to find shelter soon.

They were making their way to a cave in Sligo (*sly-go*) when they heard the grunting of a wild boar behind them. They were petrified because Diarmuid had been warned by a seer that a boar was the only deadly danger he could not face. When the boar charged, Diarmuid bravely took it on. After a mighty struggle, he killed the animal, but he was gravely wounded.

Fionn and his Fianna found Grainne trying to nurse her dying beloved. Grainne was aware that Fionn possessed the gift of healing and begged him to give Diarmuid water to drink from his hands. Fionn was still angry. He refused.

Only when his son Oisín begged him to save Diarmuid did Fionn agree. But he was still so furious that he allowed the water to slip through his fingers twice. By then, it was too late. Diarmuid died, leaving Grainne to grieve for the rest of her life.

In another version of the legend, Fionn and the couple made peace, and they lived happily near each other. After a few years, Fionn, who was still mistrustful and resentful of Diarmuid, invited Diarmuid on a boar hunt. Diarmuid was killed by a boar during the hunt, and Grainne was left a grieving widow with several children.

The Ballad of Caoilte mac Ronan

Caoilte (*keel-cha*) mac Ronan was a thin, gray man and a warrior of the Fianna. He was said to be the quickest man in all of Ireland. Caoilte was also a very loyal friend of Fionn mac Cumhaill. The Irish told a tale of how the high king asked the Fianna to bring him a bag of sand filled from all the beaches of Ireland. Many of the finest Fianna lined up before him. He asked them who could do it the quickest, and he received various answers from days to weeks to even months. When he at last reached Caoilte mac Ronan, the man replied that it would take no time at all. He had done it already while the king was still talking!

One day, there was a dispute between the high king and the Fianna that was becoming rather serious. The king asked Fionn mac Cumhaill if he would come to the palace as a hostage while they negotiated with the Fianna and the protestors who had joined them. Fionn went willingly, but when Caoilte heard that his friend and leader was being held hostage, he was furious.

Caoilte created havoc among the people. He set fire to their fields, broke into their homes, and even swapped their wives around. The king was nervous when he heard about the commotion that Caoilte was causing. What he did not know was that Caoilte had already sneaked into the palace dressed as a servant. He swapped the king's good sword with his own damaged one! Then, he stood behind the king's chair with a candle while the king and his guests were dining.

When Caoilte handed the king his glass of wine, the suspicious king mentioned to Fionn that he smelled Caoilte's skin in the wine. Caoilte knew he was caught and came forward. He asked the king what he wanted in exchange for Fionn's freedom. After some thought, the king answered that he wanted to see a pair of every creature in Ireland together in one place. He believed that would keep Caoilte busy for some time, giving the king and Fionn time to sort out the rebellion. Or so the king thought!

Caoilte had a terrible time herding all the animals together, especially the hunters and their prey. It was hard to get the deer so close to the wolves. But he was driving the herd so fast that there was no time for the animals to make mischief. By the evening, he had them in front of the gates of Tara, the seat of the high king.

The king needed more time and instructed his men to tell Caoilte that he wanted to see the animals in daylight. He gave Caoilte an enormous house with nine doors to keep the animals in until the sun rose. Poor Caoilte did not sleep a wink. He ran around all night keeping the animals from escaping or hurting each other.

The next morning, Caoilte herded the animals and birds to the plain in front of the palace. The creatures were making such a noise that the people called them "Caoilte's rabble," and that is what they called the story from then on. The king looked out over the flock and decided it was such a magnificent sight that he released Fionn.

The Fianna and the Sidhe Defend Ireland

The Battle of Ventry was a late addition to the stories of the Fenian Cycle, although it was said to have been orally passed down since the 5th century. Caoilte visited places in Ireland with Saint Patrick after Oisín's death. One day, they arrived at the hill above the Bay of Ventry, and Caoilte told Saint Patrick its legend. It is a good example of cooperation between the Irish people and the people of the Otherworld—the faeries and, in this case, the Tuatha Dé Danann.

Ventry Bay, Ireland.[36]

Dáire Donn (*daw-rah dunn*), known as the King of the World—the Fenian name for Europe—wanted to increase his lands and bring Fionn mac Cumhaill down. He had heard stories of the brave, legendary hero of Ireland, and he might have been a little jealous of his fame. When Fionn abducted the wife and daughter of one of his subject kings in France, Dáire Donn knew the time was right.

On their way to meet the invaders, Fionn and his men meet Cael (*kale*), a prince from Leinster and a friend of Fionn. They got sidetracked into helping Cael woo a blonde beauty of the Otherworld. The lady accepted Cael's proposal, and the couple got married. They both left her palace with Fionn and the Fianna to join the battle.

The battle lasted for 366 days. Cael was killed chasing an enemy into the sea, and his wife died of grief soon after. At this point, the Fianna called upon the deities of the Tuatha Dé Danann from the Otherworld for help. They agreed. The battle ended after Fionn killed Dáire Donn and a fierce Amazon warrior woman.

Caoilte told the tale in great detail to Saint Patrick, who told his scribe to record every word.

Chapter 8 Activity

Answer the questions below.

1. What is the Book of Lismore?

_____

_____

_____

_____

2. What happened when Oisín and Caoilte returned from Tír na nÓg?

_____

_____

_____

_____

3. Who are the main characters in the legend of the Giant's Causeway?

_____

_____

_____

_____

4. What happens to Diarmuid at the end of the story of Diarmuid and Grainne?

_____

_____

_____

_____

5. Who is Caoilte Mac Ronan? What is he known for?

_____

_____

_____

_____

Answers

1. The Book of Lismore or the Book of Mac Carthaig Riabhach is a manuscript written in Irish in the late 15th century for Lord Carbery, Finghean mac Carthaigh in County Cork, Ireland.

2. Oisín and Caoilte returned from Tír na nÓg to find that three hundred years had passed in their absence. They immediately turned into two incredibly old men but somehow stayed alive.

3. The legend of the Giant's Causeway involves Fionn Mac Cumhaill, a giant who had to defend Ireland against a giant from Scotland named Benandonner.

4. At the end of the story of Diarmuid and Grainne, Diarmuid is gravely wounded by a wild boar. Despite Grainne's pleas, Fionn refuses to heal Diarmuid, and he dies, leaving Grainne to grieve for the rest of her life.

5. Caoilte mac Ronan was a warrior of the Fianna. He was said to be the quickest man in all of Ireland and a very loyal friend of Fionn Mac Cumhaill.

Chapter 9: The Secrets of the Sidhe

The Sidhe (*shee*) are the faerie folk in Irish mythology. They have regained their place in Irish culture since the revival of Celtic traditions over the last few centuries. In translated literature, they are described as beautiful, ethereal beings. They resemble humans in their size and appearance, although there are a few important exceptions.

They possess wisdom, healing powers, and other supernatural powers, including shapeshifting and invisibility. They act as mediators between the natural and spiritual world. They are protectors of the natural world and the

Faerie folk or the Sidhe of Ireland.[37]

humans of Ireland. The Sidhe can cast spells, curse, or bless humans depending on their actions.

The Sidhe dwell in the Otherworld and the prehistoric tombs, caves, mounds, and hills of Ireland. They can reach the Otherworld through the passages that lead from these places. They also frequent the forests, groves, bogs, and faerie hills. The Sidhe are associated with hawthorn trees.

Faerie hills of the Sidhe.[38]

The Sidhe include the race of the Tuatha Dé Danann since the Tuatha Dé Danann were driven from Ireland by the Milesians. Some say the Sidhe are descendants of the Tuatha Dé Danann, which would mean they did not exist before the Tuatha Dé Danann moved to the Otherworld. This theory does not make sense because many stories include both races while the Tuatha Dé Danann ruled Ireland. The world of the Sidhe is also shared with the spirits of the human dead who are deemed worthy of paradise.

Their Otherworld lies to the west of Ireland, or they could be among us but in a mystical realm of space and time! They can only be seen when they choose to be seen. Some say that Ireland's faeries are only figments of the imagination of superstitious people, but in Ireland, anything is possible.

The mystical Land of Eternal Youth, Tír na nÓg, is part of the Otherworld. Everything is perfect in that realm. Everything one could ever need is there. It is a beautiful paradise in every way. The Sidhe mingle with humans on occasion, although sometimes it is to abduct or trick someone into going home with them! Ireland's myths are full of love stories between a human and a person from the Otherworld, like the story of Oisín.

If one stays out late at night on Halloween (Samhain), it is whispered that the Sidhe will entice you to dance with them and the spirits of the dead. Before you realize it, they will form a joyful, dancing circle around you and take you to their home, never to be seen again by the living.

Different Roles of the Sidhe

The Sidhe do not all look alike or display the same characteristics. They can be nice and kind or mean, so people try to stay clear of them. You never know which type will appear if you attract their attention. Let us have a look at a few of the well-known Sidhe.

- **Leprechauns** – These mischievous characters are usually portrayed as small people who play tricks on humans. They are kind creatures with the talent of a **cobbler** (*shoemaker*). They are mentioned in writings from the 700s CE. If a human can catch a leprechaun to find his gold, he will give the person three wishes for his freedom. However, he is a trickster, so he always manages to escape.

  The Irish people are protective of their leprechauns. There is even a nature preserve in Carlingford, County Louth, where the signboard literally mentions the leprechauns as one of the protected species!

  A leprechaun from an engraving from 1900.[29]

- **Banshees** – Think of eerie sounds of wailing, mournful sobbing, and screeching. That's a banshee. They take the guise of old hags who bring news of an impending death. They are said to be the spirits of the professional mourners who were hired by the Irish in ancient times to wail at funerals. They might also include women who died tragically.

According to folklore, banshees still wail before someone of the oldest Irish families passes on. So, if you are a Kavanagh, an O'Neil, O'Brien, O'Connor, or O'Grady, banshees might still be wailing for your families in Ireland!

The most famous sighting of a banshee is said to have occurred in Scotland when a banshee warned King James I of Scotland of his coming assassination in 1437.

- **Púcas** – Also called pookas, these mischievous faeries only appear at night. They are shapeshifters who can change into an animal, often a large black talking horse. They have a particular interest in men who get drunk. As a horse, they talk an unsuspecting culprit into getting on. They then take their victim for a nightmarish ride through the night. Many drunkards have apparently found themselves disheveled and aching all over at the side of a road when dawn breaks!

  There are also tales where a púca helped farmers get their crops harvested.

- **Merrows** – Mermaids in Gaelic mythology are called merrows. They are often described as the sea faeries of Ireland. Female merrows are beautiful, with flowing hair—often green—and a human-like upper body. In some tales, they have webbed fingers and greenish scales. They wear a magical cap or cloak that lets them move between sea and land. If a man hides this cloak, the merrow cannot return to the sea and may become his bride. Male merrows are said to be ugly and are typically not loved by female merrows. Merrow women sometimes enchant or lure men into the ocean.

- **Far Darrig** (*far dah-rig*) – A look-alike of leprechauns, their mischief is more malicious. They are fat little men who always wear a red coat and cap. They are the ones who replace babies with changelings. They also cause nightmares. However, they are not always bad because they reward those who are kind to them.

- **Changelings** – There are scary faeries who would swap another faerie with a human, usually a baby. Reasons vary from pure mischief or revenge, to saving a child from harsh parents, or just wanting a beautiful human baby for themselves out of envy. Sometimes, an old and tired faerie would wish to die in a loving environment, cared for by doting human parents. As a changeling, they would take on the look of the healthy human baby, while other faeries carried off the human child. The changeling would soon develop symptoms one gets when older. They would get sick and die. Other changelings would appear to develop like normal children at first, but then start to display abnormal behavior or develop strange and abnormal physical qualities. A person who behaved other than what was expected of them would often be suspected of being a changeling.

- **The Dullahan** (*dull-uh-han*) – The Dullahan is a fearsome sight! His name means "without a head," and he appears as a headless man riding a black horse. He has been known to appear as a woman on occasion. He carries his severed head under his arm. The head has piercing eyes that can see in the dark, and he has a vicious grin that goes from ear to ear. He uses a human spine as a whip, and his horse pulls a cart made of dried-out human skin. The lamps on his wagon are made from human skulls. The Dullahan was a harbinger of death and had some control over who was to die.

The Mermaid of Moher

One day, a mermaid took off her magical cloak and walked on the beach. A young man was fishing nearby. He saw her coming out of the water and where she hid her cloak.

The bold young man started a conversation with her when she approached him. She replied, and soon, they were chatting away. But the man had his eye on the rock where she had hidden her cloak. He laughed and chatted about the weather, the birds, the clouds, and everything within sight. He distracted her by pointing to all these things.

When she was looking toward the land, he dashed to the rock, grabbed her cloak, and ran for his house. He hid the cloak in a hiding place that was not easy to find. The mermaid needed her cloak to get back into the water. She had no choice. She followed him to his house but could not find the cloak.

The young man asked her to stay with him and to marry him. Again, she had no choice but to agree. They had two children—a girl and a boy. Although they were happy, the mermaid kept looking for her magic cloak.

Then, one day, she discovered where it was hidden while her husband was out fishing and the children were visiting friends. She grabbed her magic cloak and ran to the sea. Her husband was shocked when he returned home to find her gone. When he checked the hiding place and saw that her cloak was no longer there, he knew that she had gone back to the sea.

Neither he nor their children ever saw her again.

Appeasing the Sidhe

The Sidhe could bestow blessings or disasters. If any crops were left in the fields after Samhain, the púca would dry them out overnight. They were believed to do the same with berries and fruit. The Irish would leave gifts for the púca at this time to appease them so that they would not harm people.

The Irish also left other vegetables outside their homes with fearsome images carved in them to scare the púca away. They were similar to today's jack-o'-lanterns.

People also dressed up in scary disguises to confuse the Sidhe who might want to harm them. Remember, this is one of the times when it is thought that the veil between the natural world and the Otherworld is at its thinnest! The practice of putting on costumes is still followed on Halloween.

Cultural Practices to Appease the Sidhe

To appease the Sidhe, the Irish made sure that they celebrated all the festivals and left gifts out for them. People also built shrines to honor these supernatural beings. They tended to the shrines to make sure the Sidhe felt honored and not neglected.

Believers and followers of Irish paganism still follow many of these old customs. They avoid attracting attention from the Sidhe by talking softly, not damaging monuments, and not criticizing any perceived faerie actions. They do not build near mounds, faerie hills, ancient monuments, or other entrances to the Otherworld. Food items like milk, bread, and butter are left at these places on feast days.

Whistling at night or sleeping under a hawthorn tree may also attract unwanted attention from the Sidhe. Respecting nature by speaking softly and politely and avoiding areas considered likely to be frequented by the Sidhe are superstitions that people still follow today.

Chapter 9 Activity

Answer the following questions.

1. Who are the Sidhe in Irish mythology?

2. What powers do the Sidhe possess? Where do they dwell?

3. How are leprechauns portrayed in Irish mythology?

4. What are the banshees, and what is their role in Irish folklore?

5. How did the Irish people appease the Sidhe? What were some of the cultural practices associated with this?

Answers

1. The Sidhe are the faerie folk of Irish mythology. They are described as beautiful, ethereal beings. They resemble humans in size and appearance.

2. The Sidhe possess wisdom, healing powers, and other supernatural powers, including shapeshifting and invisibility. They act as intermediaries between the natural and spiritual worlds. They dwell in the Otherworld and in the prehistoric tombs, caves, mounds, and hills of Ireland.

3. Leprechauns are mischievous characters. They are usually portrayed as small people playing tricks on humans. They are also benevolent creatures with the talent of a cobbler. They are said to hide pots of gold.

4. Banshees are faeries who look like old hags. They bring news of an impending death. They are said to be the spirits of the professional mourners who were hired by the Irish in ancient times to wail at funerals.

5. To appease the Sidhe, the Irish made sure that they celebrated all the festivals and left gifts out for them. People also built shrines to honor these supernatural beings. They tended to the shrines to make sure the Sidhe felt honored and stayed happy.

Chapter 10: Folklore and Legends After Christianity

What happened to the wonderful stories of Irish mythology and folklore after the Christianization of Ireland? They were adapted, rewritten, and added to countless times up to the modern day. One part of Irish mythology that made it easy to insert additions to was the origins of the people who populated Ireland. You will recall that both the Tuatha Dé Danann and the Milesians arrived there after a lengthy journey at sea. But where did they come from? Who were their ancestors?

Map of Ireland when it was still part of the British monarchy.[80]

In this chapter, we are going to look at how the Christian monks and scribes recorded and rewrote bits and pieces of Irish oral history, folklore, myths, and legends. Some of them are the same or similar stories as recounted by the Irish to the first Christian scribes. However, the tales were written from a Christian viewpoint, and details that would make Christians uncomfortable or lead them astray from the Catholic Church were left out. Other details and even new stories were added by medieval authors, scribes, and compilers to make sense of it all.

Despite being so careful with the retelling of Ireland's myths and legends, Christian authors often used Irish and Celtic symbols in text decorations and illustrations of their manuscripts. They commonly used the Celtic cross, Celtic knots, spirals, and mythical creatures. Some magnificent examples of this mixed pagan and Christian symbolism are seen in the Book of Kells. This illuminated Christian manuscript was written around 800 CE in a British monastery. It became an Irish treasure when it was moved there for safekeeping during the Viking raids. It is currently housed in Trinity College in Dublin.

A close-up detail of an initial from the Book of Kells.[81]

Refugees from Troy

Two legends trace Irish ancestry to refugees from Troy after its fall. In one legend, they were led by Brutus, a great-grandson of Aeneas. After roaming for years, they found a large glass tower in the ocean. From the top, they could see Ireland in the distance. They went on to settle Ireland and the Isle of Man. In another version, they first settled in Iberia before moving on to Ireland.

Lebor Gabála Érenn – The Book of Invasions

Arguably, the most popular account of Irish history and mythology is the *Lebor Gabála Érenn* (*leh-vor gaw-baw-la ay-ren*). It covers the history of Ireland from the beginning of the world, according to the Christian Bible, and to the Middle Ages.

An Irish monk writing a manuscript.[22]

According to this book, which was written and compiled in the 11th century CE from earlier accounts, the first people to set foot in Ireland were Noah's descendants. They landed at Bantry Bay. The group died out except for one couple who became the ancestors of the mythical race of the Fomorians. According to other legends, they all died, and the land was uninhabited for three hundred years.

The *Lebor Gabála Érenn*'s compiler made the origins of the Irish people fit into the biblical Book of Genesis. Adam, through Noah's descendants, became the ancestor of the Irish. Legends were crafted that connected the people of Ireland to a tribe that experienced trials and tribulations like the Israelites. They migrated from place to place in search of a homeland after the Great Flood and the fall of the Tower of Babel.

Descendants of Japheth

One backstory was invented that compared Irish history with the Israelites, including their slavery in Egypt, their wanderings in the desert, and their settlement in the promised land. In the case of the Irish, they were descendants of Noah's son Japheth (*jay-feth*). They spent time in Greece as slaves, escaped, and sailed the seas for years before finding their promised land—Ireland. In another version, these descendants of Noah spent time in Egypt under a pharaoh's control before roaming for years through the desert. They mixed with the Scythians from the Eurasian Steppe (*grasslands*) before settling in Iberia and then Ireland.

The Story of Goídel

The genealogy is a little different in *The Book of Invasions*. In it, one of Japheth's descendants, a Scythian prince, took part in building the Tower of Babel. After the confusion of languages, his grandson, Goídel Glas (*goy-duhl glass*), constructed the Goidelic or Gaelic language.

Goídel, a Scythian, lived in Egypt. His father was married to an Egyptian princess. The family prospered, and their numbers grew in Egypt for a time until they were exiled by the pharaoh. Their exile happened at the same time as the biblical Exodus of the Israelites. This legend says that Moses predicted that Goídel and his wife, who was also an Egyptian princess, would discover and settle in Ireland. Goídel knew Moses because Moses had cured him from a deadly snakebite by laying his staff on the wound. The wound left a green mark on Goídel for the rest of his life.

Goídel and his descendants roamed the world for 440 years. They experienced many hardships during this time. Eventually, they settled in the Iberian Peninsula in Spain. They lived there for more than a thousand years.

A direct descendant of Goídel, Breogan (*bray-oh-gawn*), founded a new city there. He built a high tower overlooking the ocean. His son, Íth (Íoth in some versions), saw the lush green hills of Ireland from the top of this tower. The tribe, which had grown to become very large, decided to move to Ireland.

In another version of the story, the group that moves into Ireland is the original group led by Goídel and his Egyptian wife. The period of roaming the earth and settling in Iberia was much shorter. Or they were possibly descendants with the same names as the original Goídel and his Egyptian wife. They became the ancestors of today's Irish people.

A later story from the 15th century by a Scottish author named Walter Bower makes Goídel's wife, Scota, the founder of the Scots.

Scota and Goídel on their way to Scotland. A drawing from the manuscript of Walter Bower.⁸⁸

Partholón

The leader of the next group of settlers was a group under Partholón, a descendant of Magog, who was descended from Noah. Partholón is Old Irish for the name Bartholomew.

They arrived in Ireland after spending time in Greece, Anatolia (Turkey), Sicily, and Spain. The island was wild, thickly forested, and empty when they arrived. There was only one cleared valley for planting crops. Water was limited to three lakes and nine rivers.

They set about clearing four more fields, and miraculously, seven new lakes sprang forth from the ground. During their travels to Ireland, they learned many new skills, including metalworking and farming. They introduced the domestication of plants and animals. They bred cattle, plowed and harvested crops, and brewed beer.

The Fomorians from the Isle of Man constantly raided and attacked them. According to some interpretations of the ancient texts, the Fomorians were a group of evil supernatural beings who caused droughts, floods, and other disasters.

Partholón's descendants increased, and eventually, they were able to defeat the Fomorians in battle. However, they would not survive for much longer. Pestilence broke out on their beautiful island, and in one week, they all died. Only one person survived so that their story could be told.

Nemed

Again, Ireland was left uninhabited, this time for thirty years. After that, the third group of people arrived. They were led by Nemed (*nev-ed*), another descendant of Noah. They left their home near the Caspian Sea with forty-four ships, but only the ship that carried Nemed, his family, and companions made it to the shores of Ireland.

They were a busy lot! They cleared twelve more fields and built two forts. They were rewarded with four more lakes. Meanwhile, the annoying Fomorians started their raids again. They were beaten back in four battles. But Nemed's numbers were depleted by the plague. Nemed was one of its victims. In the next battle, the Fomorians were the victors.

The Nemedians were forced to pay two-thirds of everything to the Fomorians every Samhain. This included their children, their harvests, and their animals. When they rebelled against the Fomorians with a large force, they killed one of the Fomorian leaders. The other leader destroyed the Nemedian forces. Those who were not killed in battle were swallowed by the sea.

One ship with thirty men on board escaped the carnage. They fled to Britain, Greece, and the mysterious north. The descendants of those who went to Greece returned after 230 years. They were the Fir Bolg. They divided Ireland into five provinces, each with a king. Nine high kings ruled in succession over the whole of Ireland for thirty-seven years from the Hill of Tara.

Those who went north came back as the next invaders, the mystical race of the Tuatha Dé Danann. They ruled Ireland for 150 years. After them came the Milesians, who became the Irish people we know today.

Kings' Lists of Ireland

The last cycle of Irish mythology is known as the Kings' Cycle or the Historical Cycle. The *Lebor Gabála Érenn* lists the high kings of Ireland starting around 2000 BCE. Most of the early kings up to around the 6th century CE are believed to be fictional. From the time of the Tuatha Dé Danann (around 1800 BCE), the kings were crowned at the sacred Hill of Tara.

You may recall that the Tuatha Dé Danann brought four magical gifts with them to Ireland. One of these was the Lia Fáil (*lee-uh fawl*), or the Stone of Destiny. According to legend, this was the magical stone on which the kings were crowned. The stone would cry out a joyful roar when the rightful king set foot on it. If the new king was a **usurper** (*not the rightful heir*), the stone remained quiet!

The Lia Fáil lost its power after Cú Chulainn split it with his sword when it did not acknowledge Cú Chulainn's pick for king. It was said to have reacted only twice after that. The last time was with the crowning of Brian Boru in 1002 CE.

Like the Ulster and Fenian cycles, the Kings' Cycle contains a blend of mythology and history. In the *Lebor Gabála Érenn*, there are definite links to real kings in the latter parts of the list. The compiler even linked some of their timelines to those of other

An Irish king from Myths and Legends.[34]

countries like Egypt. Overall, it is a long and boring list, so we will look at only a few of the kings who had interesting tales.

Labraid Loingsech (*lou-rid lung-shekh*)

Labraid Loingsech's uncle killed Labraid's grandfather and father and usurped the throne of the high king. He banished Labraid. Labraid took refuge in France, where he became famous as one of the king's personal guards. He even married the king's daughter. He made peace with his uncle in Ireland after thirty long years.

Upon his return to Ireland, Labraid was given the province of Leinster. However, the peace with his uncle, Cobthach (*kub-hakh*), did not last. War broke out. Labraid invited Cobthach and thirty other Irish kings to a feast to make peace. When Cobthach and the other guests, including Labraid's mother and the court jester, were inside the building, Labraid locked the door and set the house on fire.

They all burned to death, as Labraid had the house built of iron. His mother and the jester knew of his plan but sacrificed themselves willingly for him. The visitors would not have entered the house without them since they had all felt uneasy about the invitation.

Labraid was also said to have been born with long ears like those of a horse. He kept his hair long to cover his shame. Once a year, when his hair was trimmed, the barber would be killed afterward so that he could not tell anybody. Labraid spared one barber after the barber's mother pleaded with him not to kill her only son. The barber was so obsessed with the king's secret that it made him ill. He consulted a Druid, who told him to tell the secret to the first tree he came to after the nearby crossroad. The barber did as the Druid had told him. The first tree he encountered after the crossroad was a beautiful willow. He told the willow tree all about the king's shame and felt immediate relief.

A short while later, the king's harpist had an accident in which he broke his harp. He used wood from that same willow tree at the crossroad to make a new harp. Every time he played the new harp, the wood cried out for all to hear that the king had horse ears. Labraid admitted his secret and repented for all the poor barbers that he had killed.

In another tale, Saint Brigid fixed his ears. Labraid had to lay his head on her lap, and she fixed his problem by gently rubbing his ears.

Suibne mac Colmain – the Mad King

Suibne mac Colmain (*siv-nya mac kull-wawn*) was the king of the Dál nAraidi (*dawl na-rah-dja*) near County Down and County Antrim in today's Ireland. He went crazy after he was cursed by Saint Rónán Finn to wander around naked and in complete madness across Ireland. But what did he do to deserve this curse?

Saint Rónán was marking off a piece of ground to build a new church. The sound of the bell hanging from the priest's neck alerted Suibne. He was informed that the saint was preparing to build a church on his land. Suibne was enraged. He ran for the door, covered only by his cloak. His wife tried to stop him by grabbing onto his cloak. The cloak unraveled, and he went after the saint stark naked.

Reaching the saint, Suibne grabbed his psalter (Book of Psalms) and threw it into the lake. Then, he tried to drag the saint away. He was interrupted by a message from the high king, which told him to join the nearby Battle of Mag Rath immediately. The priest cursed Suibne, saying that he would go crazy, wander the earth, and be killed by a spear. The next day, an otter brought the psalter back to the saint.

The saint was also involved in the battle. He negotiated a truce between the parties. They agreed to stop fighting every day at dusk and start fighting again at daybreak. He blessed the troops with holy water each evening and ensured the opponents did not breach the truce.

The hot-headed Suibne regularly broke this pact. One evening, when Saint Rónán was going around blessing the troops by sprinkling them with holy water, Suibne suddenly decided it was an insult when the holy water was sprinkled on him. Suibne killed Saint Rónán's companion with a spear. His second spear got stuck in the priest's metal bell. After this, the saint repeated the curse, and Suibne became crazy. He left the battlefield and tried to perch on a tree like a bird.

He fled from tree to tree across the countryside for years. He even wandered to Scotland and Britain. At times when he was lucid, he returned to Ireland. In the end, Suibne was killed by the spear of a jealous husband. The man saw his wife feeding the crazy fellow and thought that Suibne was trying to steal his wife away from him.

Cormac mac Airt – The Best of Kings

High King Cormac mac Airt of Ireland was king during the Fenian Cycle. He was the creator of the Fianna. He is said to have reigned for forty years, during which time Ireland was peaceful and prosperous. He was admired and adored by his people as a just and fair ruler.

Cormac mac Airt's father had been overthrown and killed by a usurper before he was born. His mother was the daughter of a Druid. He was raised in secret to protect him from his father's enemies. Legends about his childhood and youth said he was raised by a pack of wild wolves. Cormac mac Airt's wisdom, knowledge, and justice indicate that his Druid grandfather had a hand in raising him, not wild animals!

After Cormac mac Airt learned about his heritage, he went to Tara to reclaim his father's throne. He won the support of the people and nobles with his courteous manners. The time was right for him to challenge the usurper, Mac Con, for the throne. The rightful high king reclaimed his father's throne after a victorious battle. Mac Con and his men were forced to flee.

Stories of his legendary wisdom were influenced by the Christian monks who recorded the oral folktales. One particular legend is closely based on the biblical story of Solomon. Two men were fighting over the ownership of a special sword. They brought the matter to King Cormac.

After listening to both sides, he ordered the sword to be split into equal halves so that each contender would receive an exact share. One man immediately gave up his claim to save the sword from being destroyed. Cormac, realizing the man's true feelings for the sword, gave it unbroken to him.

In another legend, Cormac mac Airt was asked for advice by three men who wanted to know how to live a good life. He advised fairness, justice, and moderation to be the basis of all things. He is also said to have taught his people many proverbs, just like the biblical Solomon!

Ireland was said to have prospered under the rule of Cormac mac Airt. He was remembered as a wise and fair king who helped shape the country's ancient legal system, called Brehon Law. This law code focused on making things right rather than punishing people harshly. A person's rights and responsibilities depended on their social rank. While many people could own land, what they could own or inherit often depended on their status. Brehons, or judges, were chosen because they were known to be fair and didn't take sides. Cormac mac Airt became famous for his smart and fair decisions.

He is credited with establishing a school of law for judges and a school of Druidry. He is also credited with building many structures on the Hill of Tara, including a banquet hall, his house, and Gráinne's enclosure, which was dedicated to his daughter. He held feasts and gatherings for poets and artists at Tara.

After ruling for forty years, Cormac mac Airt lost one of his eyes. The reasons for this mishap vary. It might have been caused by an accident when a spear point hit him by chance. It might have been cut out on purpose by his enemy, Angus. Cormac had to abdicate the throne since the Irish believed that a king with any disability would bring bad luck to the people. Cormac gave his crown and his palace to his son, Cairbre, and left Tara. It is said that he spent the rest of his life on a nearby hill, where he used his wisdom and knowledge to perfect the Brehon Laws that governed Ireland for generations to come.

Cormac mac Airt became the inspiration for poets, songwriters, and artists for centuries. He represented the ideal king for future generations of the Irish. It has become quite a task to sort legends and myths of Cormac mac Airt from historical facts since great abilities, deeds, and magical experiences were added in every retelling!

Even in death, Cormac mac Airt's story presents us with a puzzle. According to some versions, Cormac mac Airt believed in one God of heaven and earth—and this was before the time of Saint Patrick and Christianization. A group of Druids tried to force him to kneel and dance with them and their followers around a golden idol. When he refused, they cursed him. Shortly thereafter, he died from choking on a salmon bone.

However, this was too unfair a death in the minds of the Irish people for such an exalted king, and it reflected badly on the Druids, who were still held in high regard at that time. To have Cormac mac Airt gently moving on and joining the faeries and the gods in the Otherworld seemed more appropriate.

So, myths and legends were adapted, and new ones were added. Stories spread that said Cormac, as an old man, just suddenly vanished. He disappeared one day, never to be seen again! He could be forever young and healthy in Tír na nÓg, enjoying peace and happiness in paradise after being a just and wise king of Ireland.

Chapter 10 Activity

Answer the following questions. Remember, if you get stuck, you can always reread the chapter to find the right answer. You can also check the back of the book for sample answers.

1. What happened to the stories of Irish mythology and folklore after the Christianization of Ireland?

_____

_____

_____

2. According to the Lebor Gabála Érenn, who were the first people to set foot in Ireland? What happened to them?

_____

_____

_____

3. Who is Goídel, and what is his significance in Irish mythology?

_____

_____

_____

4. What is the Lia Fáil, and what role did it play in the crowning of kings?

_____

_____

_____

5. Who was Suibne Mac Colmain, and why was he known as the Mad King?

_____

_____

_____

Answers

1. The stories of Irish mythology and folklore were adapted, rewritten, and added to countless times up to the modern day after the Christianization of Ireland.

2. According to the Lebor Gabála Érenn, the first people to set foot in Ireland were Noah's descendants. They landed at Bantry Bay. The group died out except for one couple who became the forefathers of the mythical race of the Fomorians. According to other legends, they all died, and the land was uninhabited for three hundred years.

3. Goídel is one of Japheth's descendants whose grandfather took part in the building of the Tower of Babel. After the confusion of languages in the biblical Book of Genesis, Goídel constructed the Goidelic or Gaelic language. Goídel lived in Egypt. In another version, his mother was an Egyptian princess. They were exiled by a later pharaoh and ended up in Spain and then Ireland.

4. The Lia Fáil, also known as the "Stone of Destiny," is one of the four magical gifts brought to Ireland by the Tuatha Dé Danann. According to legend, this was the magical stone on which the kings were crowned. The stone would cry out a joyful roar when the rightful king set foot on it.

5. Suibne mac Colmain, also known as the Mad King, was king of the Dál nAraidi near County Down and County Antrim in today's Ireland. He went crazy after he was cursed by Saint Ronan Finn to wander around naked and in complete madness across Ireland.

Bonus Chapter: Legendary Figures in Irish History

Irish history is filled with legendary figures whose stories have been passed down through the centuries. Some of these people definitely lived, while others are known only through myth and folklore. In this chapter, we'll explore four fascinating figures from Ireland's past. Each of them left a mark on Irish storytelling—some through historical achievements, others through magical tales. As you read, ask yourself which of these figures really walked the earth and which ones might only live in legend.

Grace O'Malley – Legendary Pirate Queen

Grace O'Malley is the Anglicized name of Gráinne Ní Mháille (*grawn-ya nee wall-ya*). Grace was a real person who lived during the 16th century. However, her story is filled with so many legends and folk tales that it is hard to know what is true and what isn't. She is seen as a symbol of courage and resistance in many parts of Ireland. Most of what is known about her today comes from folk tales rather than history books. She is not mentioned in Ireland's official records, but her basic information is preserved in Queen Elizabeth I's annals.

A statue of Grace O'Malley.⁸⁵

Grace inherited her wealthy father's castles, dockyards, fleet of trading ships, and land along the west coast of Ireland. Like her father, she demanded tribute from ships sailing through her part of the coastal waters.

Grace often accompanied her father on trading voyages, which included trips to France and Spain. Her father initially refused to take her with him when she first asked as a small girl. His excuse was that her long hair might get tangled in the sails, ropes, and other deck equipment. Grace immediately cut off all her hair, earning her the nickname

"Gráinne Mhaol" (bald Grace). He could no longer refuse her request after she did this. Grace was a seasoned sailor and skipper by the time she was a teenager.

Although she was rebellious and refused to conform to traditional feminine norms, Grace was married at sixteen to the son and heir of an equally wealthy clan, the O'Flaherty family. Grace had three children— one girl and two boys. According to some sources, she had four children. One day, her husband was murdered while hunting, and the rival clan that killed him attacked his castle. They thought it would be an easy victory since a woman was in charge of the defense. The livid Grace viciously drove them off. The O'Flaherty's castle became known as Hen's Castle because of Grace's fierce defense.

Grace moved her headquarters back to her childhood home, the stronghold of the O'Malleys on Clare Island. It was now called Granuaile Castle after Grace. The O'Flaherty men fully accepted Grace as their leader and followed her.

Grace O'Malley became feared and respected along the west coast as a pirate queen. She led raids against rival clans and sometimes English merchant ships, commanding a fleet of ships and loyal seafarers. She controlled important sea routes and demanded tribute from any ship passing through her waters. Those who refused often faced attack. Her strongholds at Clew Bay and Achill Island gave her strategic power over trade and travel. English officials, including Sir Richard Bingham, accused her of piracy, but Grace saw herself as a protector of her people's land and livelihood. Her maritime empire became one of the last strongholds of Irish resistance during Elizabethan rule.

However, it was a time of unrest in Ireland. England was claiming its soil and its people. Irish lords were pitted against each other. Some were in favor of England's rule, and others wanted to fiercely guard Ireland's independence.

The local English lord deputy of Ireland arrested dissidents, including some of Grace's family. She set sail for England to negotiate directly with Queen Elizabeth. It is said that Grace refused to bow when she was allowed to meet the queen. Grace considered them equals. The two well-educated women conducted their meeting in private. By the end of the meeting, Elizabeth agreed to release Grace's family and leave her and her clan alone in the future.

Grace O'Malley is commemorated by the Irish. The name "Granuaile" has been given to parks, ships, and boats. Songs, poems, and various literature mention her, with the most famous being several books written by author Anne Chambers.

Brian Boru – The High King of Ireland

Brian Boru was born around 941 in the Kingdom of Thomond, part of modern-day County Clare. He belonged to a rising family in the Dál gCais (dawl gahsh) tribe. At the time, Ireland was divided into many small kingdoms, which were often at war with each other. Norse Vikings had established strongholds in coastal cities like Dublin, Limerick, and Waterford. Though they sometimes raided the countryside, they also traded and settled. Brian's older brother, Mahon, became king of Munster, but he was killed by rivals. Brian avenged his brother's death and took his place, beginning a long campaign to unite the fractured kingdoms of Ireland.

Brian wasn't content with ruling just Munster. He battled rival Irish kings and Viking forces, expanding his power. By 1002, he was recognized as high king of Ireland. This meant that he had influence over most of the island's regional rulers. Unlike many kings before him, Brian didn't come from the ancient ruling dynasty of Tara. His rise to power was extraordinary and challenged the traditional way kings were chosen in Ireland.

Brian also worked to reform the Irish Church and promoted learning and scholarship. He supported the construction of monasteries and churches. He also encouraged the use of written law. Many legends say that he brought peace and prosperity to Ireland and united the clans under one banner. Though this unity was temporary, his leadership left a powerful legacy.

The most famous moment in Brian's life came in 1014 at the Battle of Clontarf near Dublin. A massive coalition of his enemies—including the king of Leinster and Viking warriors from Dublin and abroad—rose up to challenge him. Brian's forces won the battle, but Brian was killed in his tent by retreating Viking fighters. He was over seventy years old at the time.

Over the centuries, Brian Boru became a symbol of Irish resistance and national pride. Stories about him often portray him as the king who drove the Vikings out of Ireland once and for all, though in reality, Viking communities remained for many years after. His descendants, the

O'Briens, went on to become one of the most powerful families in Ireland. Today, Brian is remembered as one of Ireland's most legendary leaders. He might not have united the whole island, but he dared to imagine that it was possible.

An 18th-century illustration of Brian Boru.[86]

Gobán Saor – Master Craftsman

Gobán Saor—whose name means "the free builder" or "builder extraordinaire"—is a legendary Irish craftsman and architect. He is believed to have lived around the 7th century.

According to folklore, he could craft churches, towers, forts, palaces, and beautiful objects from any material—metal, wood, or stone. He appears in stories as clever, witty, generous, and quick to outwit anyone who tries to cheat him. One tale tells how monks who tried to short-change him by stealing his ladder ended up paying full price after he built a ramp out of the stones that had been thrown from the tower.

In one of the most famous legends about Gobán Saor, he was hired by a powerful and arrogant king from another land to build a magnificent fort or palace. The structure was so impressive that the king became jealous. He decided that once Gobán completed the work, he would have him killed so no one else could have such an amazing builder.

But Gobán suspected the king's plan. To escape the trap, he told the king he needed a special tool to finish the job. This was actually a coded message to his wife, warning her of danger. The king sent his own son to fetch the tool, not realizing he was walking into a trap himself. When the son arrived, Gobán's wife held the prince hostage until Gobán and their son were safely home.

Some church writings from the 6th and 7th centuries mention a Saint Gobban or Gobhan. This saint is sometimes identified with Gobán Saor, but most scholars believe Gobán's adventures were mostly legendary, though he was perhaps based on a real early craftsman.

Tadhg mac Céin – The Forgotten Hero

Tadhg mac Céin (*tige mac kane*) was a legendary warrior in early Irish stories. He was a brave and clever fighter who served under kings, stood by friends in battle, and left behind a name that echoed through the halls of ancient bardic poetry. His tales might not be as widely known as those of Cú Chulainn or Fionn mac Cumhaill, but they are just as rich. While the magical parts of his story are clearly myth, some believe that Tadhg might have been based on a real historical warrior whose deeds were remembered and retold for centuries.

According to legend, Tadhg was the grandson of the king of Munster. His father, Cian, was killed by three brothers from the powerful Mac Con dynasty. After this loss, Tadhg grew up determined to prove himself, not only as a warrior but as a man of honor. He is best known from the saga *Cath Maige Mucrama* (*Battle of Mag Mucrama*), where he fights alongside Art mac Cuinn, the high king of Ireland, against the forces of Mac Con. In this battle, Tadhg's skill, bravery, and loyalty help turn the tide. He fights not for fame or fortune but for friendship and what he believes is right.

Another story, *Eachtra Thaidg Mhic Céin* (*Adventures of Tadhg mac Céin*), tells of his magical journeys and battles in distant lands. He faces giants, beasts, and even strange spells, always managing to overcome danger with a mix of courage and cleverness. In one tale, he goes on a nearly impossible quest to rescue a kidnapped noblewoman and faces tests of strength, wit, and honor. Through it all, he shows that a true hero is not just powerful but also faithful and kind.

Tadhg mac Céin stands out in Irish stories because he isn't the strongest or most famous, but he is unshakably loyal, deeply honorable, and willing to risk everything to help his allies. His name doesn't appear in history books, but some scholars believe he might have been inspired by a real warrior from ancient Munster whose legacy lived on in oral traditions. Over time, stories about him became grander and more magical, but they likely started with someone who truly existed and made an impact on the people of his time.

Today, Tadhg mac Céin is a reminder that not every hero has to be a king or a god. Sometimes, the ones who fight hardest and remain the most loyal are the ones we remember longest, even if their names are forgotten.

Conclusion

During this small peek into Irish mythology, you may have noticed that the tales took you to various areas in Ireland. You are right if you guessed that many of these myths, legends, and heroes were only known in the areas where they originated. They spread over time by traveling bards (poets, musicians, and storytellers), who told the stories wherever they went. That is also the main reason why there are so many different versions of the same story.

A good example is how Fionn mac Cumhaill became the leader of the Fianna during the Fenian Cycle. Another example can be found in Cú Chulainn's tale during the Ulster Cycle. His mother is either Deichtine or Deichtire, and she is either the king of Ulster's sister or his daughter, depending on which version of the story you read. And then, there are the tales of Lugh, which pop up in several stories, places, and eras. He is sometimes a deity amongst the Tuatha Dé Danann and has the Spear of Victory. Other times, he was born in Ireland from the union of a Fomorian princess and a human king.

Another intriguing part of mythology, specifically Irish mythology, is when one tries to figure out which of the legendary heroes are based on real people. Today, gossip and sensational headlines are added to news to catch attention. Imagine how Irish mythology and heroic legends could have grown, spread, and gone viral if social media existed in ancient times!

The legends woven around heroes like Fionn mac Cumhaill and Cú Chulainn illustrate the high value placed on selfless courage. The Irish prized honor, bravery, and loyalty, and these great heroes had all of that, although they were not perfect. The willingness of both Fand and Emer to sacrifice their love for Cú Chulainn's happiness also illustrates that same selfless courage.

The story of Saint Brigid is based on a real person, but many miracles ascribed to her, like the well appearing suddenly in the ground, sound more like myths that belong to the pagan goddess Brigid. It is a good example of how pagan tales became intertwined with actual events and figures in history. The festival of Imbolc, which takes place midway between the summer and winter solstices, is celebrated on February 1st. Imbolc used to be held to celebrate the pagan goddess Brigid once they witnessed the first signs of the end of winter. Back then, this day did not fall on the same day every year, but it usually occurred close to the beginning of February. After Saint Brigid died, the festival was moved to her death date, February 1st. Every year, Imbolc is held to celebrate her life and the closeness of spring.

A good example of the confusion with lifespans and genealogies appears in the myths of the Morrigan. The Dagda and the first king of the Tuatha Dé Danann, Nuada, were both sons of the same ancient mother goddess, Danu, long before the mythological race even arrived in Ireland. The Morrigan is the wife of the Dagda. However, she is also the great-granddaughter of the Dagda's brother, King Nuada, three generations later! This clearly illustrates that people should not be analytical if they want to enjoy the wonderful stories of mythology.

The Fianna and other Irish mythological figures are widely used in films, books, video games, and comic books. Here are just a few if you would like to see how some characters or groups have been used:

- *The Secret of Kells* is a 2009 movie based on the Book of Kells, a 1,200-year-old Irish manuscript kept in the Old Library of Trinity College, Dublin.
- *Song of the Sea* is a 2014 movie about Irish mermaids and selkies.
- *Wolfwalkers* is a 2020 film based on Irish legends.
- *The Hound of Ulster* by Rosemary Sutcliff is a book about Cú Chulainn's legend.
- *Assassin's Creed: Valhalla* "Wrath of the Druids" is a video game expansion pack that includes the Children of Danu, who are the Tuatha Dé Danann in Irish mythology.

Let us conclude with the last words from a poem by the great Irish Nobel Prize-winning poet, William Butler Yeats, who loved Irish history and mythology.

"To the Rose upon the Rood of Time"

("Rose" symbolizes Ireland, and "rood" means the suffering on the cross.)

"Come near; I would, before my time to go,

Sing of old Eire, and the ancient ways:

Red Rose, proud Rose, sad Rose of all my days."[1]

---

[1] William Butler Yeats. "To the Rose upon the Rood of Time." The Poetry Foundation. https://www.poetryfoundation.org/poems/43280/to-the-rose-upon-the-rood-of-time

Here's another book by Enthralling History that you might like

Free limited time bonus

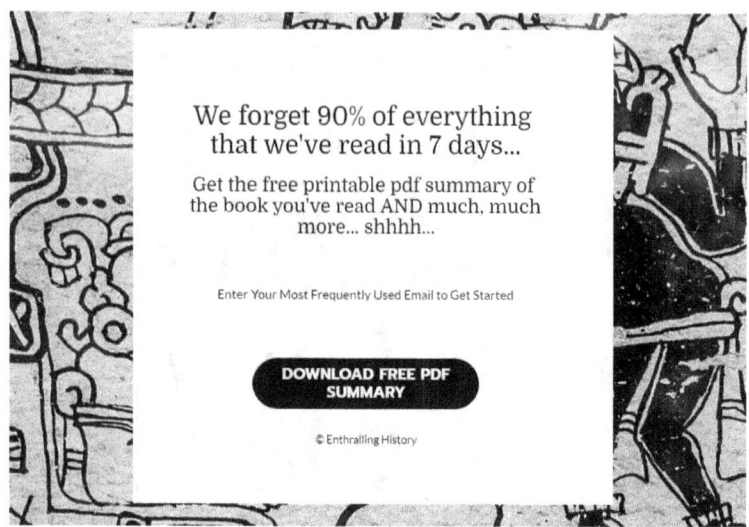

Stop for a moment. We have a free bonus set up for you. The problem is this: we forget 90% of everything that we read after 7 days. Crazy fact, right? Here's the solution: we've created a printable, 1-page pdf summary for this book that you're reading now. All you have to do to get your free pdf summary is to go to the following website:
https://livetolearn.lpages.co/enthrallinghistory/

Or, Scan the QR code!

Once you do, it will be intuitive. Enjoy, and thank you!

Bibliography

Curtin, J. (Original text 1890). *Myths and Folklore of Ireland.* (P. B. redacted., Editor) Retrieved March 2024, from Internet Sacred Texts Archive: https://sacred-texts.com/cat/srchsubj.htm?search_str=Irish+Mythology

Green, M. (Ed.). (n.d.). ARTICLES ABOUT IRELAND - HISTORY. *Ireland-Site, Ireland-Information.* Retrieved April 2024, from https://www.ireland-information.com/articlesindex.htm

Kennedy, P. (1891). Legendary Fictions of The Irish Celts. In P. Kennedy, *Legendary Fictions of the Irish Celts.* London: Macmillan & Co. Retrieved April 2024, from https://www.askaboutireland.ie/reading-room/digital-book-collection/digital-books-by-subject/folklore-of-ireland/kennedy-legendary-fiction/

Lloyd, E. (2018, April 7). Elusive Celtic Otherworld where ... *Ancient Pages Newsletter.* Retrieved April 2024, from https://www.ancientpages.com/2018/04/07/elusive-celtic-otherworld-where-tuatha-de-danann-reside-and-time-passes-slower/#googl

Murphy, M. (2003 - 2008). *Index to Lebor Cabala Erenn.* Retrieved March 2024, from Celt - Corpus of Electronic Texts: https://celt.ucc.ie/indexLG.html

Mythology, B. (n.d.). *Mythological Cycle Stories.* Retrieved April 2024, from bardmythologies.com/mythic-history-of-ireland/: https://bardmythologies.com/mythological-cycle-stories/

Staff, I. C. (2022, December 19). (I. Staff, Ed.) *Irish Central Newsletter.* Retrieved April 2024, from https://www.irishcentral.com/roots/history/history-irelands-ancient-druids

Sullivan, A. (1900). Story of Ireland. In P. Joyce, *Atlas and Cyclopedia of Ireland.* Books Ulster. Retrieved March 2024, from https://www.libraryireland.com/Atlas/Irish-History.php

Various. (n.d.). King Cormac mac Airt. *Emerald Isle*. Retrieved from https://emeraldisle.ie/king-cormac-mac-art

Various. (n.d.). *Myths and Legends*. Retrieved March/April 2024, from Irish History: https://www.irishhistory.com/myths-legends/

YouTube Videos about Irish Myths and Legends:

The Secrets Of Ancient Ireland's Celtic Mythology | Celtic Legends | Chronicle https://www.youtube.com/watch?v=9611sFF1rWI

Who is Brigid, the EXALTED one | Celtic Mythology Explained | Irish Mythology Explained. https://www.youtube.com/watch?v=cPqmmbCH4

Who Were The Irish Gods | EXPLAINED. https://www.youtube.com/watch?v=DhYC-7emtOM

Who Are the Tuatha Dé Danann? https://www.youtube.com/watch?v=jftP9CYmQDI

Image Sources

1 August Schwerdfeger, CC BY 4.0 <https://creativecommons.org/licenses/by/4.0>, via Wikimedia Commons, https://commons.wikimedia.org/wiki/File:Stone_of_Destiny_2018-07-24.jpg
2 https://commons.wikimedia.org/wiki/File:The_Fomorians,_Duncan_1912.jpg
3 Internet Archive Book Images, No restrictions, via Wikimedia Commons, https://commons.wikimedia.org/wiki/File:Myths_and_legends;_the_Celtic_race_(19 10)_(14760459036).jpg
4 https://commons.wikimedia.org/wiki/File:Riders_of_th_Sidhe_(big).jpg
5 WordRidden, CC BY 2.0 <https://creativecommons.org/licenses/by/2.0>, via Wikimedia Commons, https://commons.wikimedia.org/wiki/File:Newgrange,_Ireland_001.jpg
6 https://commons.wikimedia.org/wiki/File:Salmon-of-Knoweldge-1904.jpg
7 https://commons.wikimedia.org/w/index.php?curid=7384071)
8 Internet Archive Book Images, No restrictions, via Wikimedia Commons, https://commons.wikimedia.org/wiki/File:Myths_and_legends;_the_Celtic_race_(19 10)_(14783467965).jpg
9 Internet Archive Book Images, No restrictions, via Wikimedia Commons, https://commons.wikimedia.org/wiki/File:Myths_and_legends;_the_Celtic_race_(19 10)_(14780315151).jpg
10 William Murphy, CC BY-SA 2.0 <https://creativecommons.org/licenses/by-sa/2.0>, via Wikimedia Commons, https://commons.wikimedia.org/wiki/File:Tain_Bo_Cuailnge_Mural_(Desmond_Kinney)_(cropped).jpg
11 Leandro Neumann Ciuffo, CC BY 2.0 <https://creativecommons.org/licenses/by/2.0>, via Wikimedia Commons,

https://commons.wikimedia.org/wiki/File:Desmond_Kinney%E2%80%99s_mosaic_(6179099398).jpg

12 Internet Archive Book Images, No restrictions, via Wikimedia Commons, https://commons.wikimedia.org/wiki/File:Myths_and_legends;_the_Celtic_race_(1910)_(14596798099).jpg

13 jenniferboyer, CC BY 2.0 <https://creativecommons.org/licenses/by/2.0>, via Wikimedia Commons, https://commons.wikimedia.org/wiki/File: C%C3%BAchulainn_statue.jpg

14 https://commons.wikimedia.org/wiki/File:Saint_Brigid_by_Patrick_Joseph_Tuohy.jpg

15 https://commons.wikimedia.org/w/index.php?curid=545341

16 https://commons.wikimedia.org/wiki/File:Morrigan.jpg

17 https://commons.wikimedia.org/wiki/File:Macha.jpg

18 Internet Archive Book Images, No restrictions, via Wikimedia Commons, https://commons.wikimedia.org/wiki/File:Myths_and_legends;_the_Celtic_race_(1910)_(14780316811).jpg

19 https://commons.wikimedia.org/wiki/File:An_Arch_Druid_in_His_Judicial_Habit.jpg

20 https://commons.wikimedia.org/wiki/File:Druids_Inciting_the_Britons_to_Oppose_the_Landing_of_the_Romans.jpg

21 sandyraidy, CC BY-SA 2.0 <https://creativecommons.org/licenses/by-sa/2.0>, via Wikimedia Commons, https://commons.wikimedia.org/wiki/File: Druids_celebrating_at_Stonehenge_(0).png

22 https://commons.wikimedia.org/wiki/File:Lives_of_saints,_from_the_Book_of_Lismore_(Stokes,_1890)_frontispiece.jpg

23 Internet Archive Book Images, No restrictions, via Wikimedia Commons, https://commons.wikimedia.org/wiki/File:Myths_and_legends;_the_Celtic_race_(1910)_(14760478416).jpg

24 code poet on Flickr, CC BY-SA 2.0 <https://creativecommons.org/licenses/by-sa/2.0>, via Wikimedia Commons, https://commons.wikimedia.org/wiki/File:Causeway-code_poet-4.jpg

25 https://commons.wikimedia.org/wiki/File:The_book_of_romance_-_b%26w_plate_facing_page_216.png

26 Stream on Ventry Strand by Oliver Dixon, CC BY-SA 2.0 <https://creativecommons.org/licenses/by-sa/2.0>, via Wikimedia Commons, https://commons.wikimedia.org/wiki/File:Stream_on_Ventry_Strand_-_geograph.org.uk_-_4668342.jpg

27 Internet Archive Book Images, No restrictions, via Wikimedia Commons, https://commons.wikimedia.org/wiki/File:Heroes_of_the_dawn_(1914)_(14566143070).jpg

28 黃逸樂（世界首窮）, CC BY 3.0 <https://creativecommons.org/licenses/by/3.0>, via Wikimedia Commons, https://commons.wikimedia.org/wiki/File: Fairy_Hill_2012_-_panoramio.jpg

29 https://commons.wikimedia.org/wiki/File:Leprechaun_engraving_1900.jpg

30 https://commons.wikimedia.org/wiki/File:The_British_monarchy-_or,_a_new_chorographical_description_of_all_the_dominions_subject_to_the_King_of_Great_Britain_Fleuron_T088513-15.png

31 https://commons.wikimedia.org/wiki/File:KellsDecoratedInitial.jpg

32 https://commons.wikimedia.org/wiki/File:Irish_monk_writing.jpg

33 https://commons.wikimedia.org/wiki/File:Scota_%26_Gaedel_Glas.jpg

34 Internet Archive Book Images, No restrictions, via Wikimedia Commons, https://commons.wikimedia.org/wiki/File:Myths_and_legends;_the_Celtic_race_(1910)_(14596762680).jpg

35 Suzanne Mischyshyn / County Mayo - Westport House Grounds - Statue of Grace O'Malley (1530-1603), https://commons.wikimedia.org/wiki/File:Grainne_Mhaol_Ni_Mhaille_Statue.jpg

36 https://commons.wikimedia.org/wiki/File:Brian_B%C3%B3ruma_mac_Cenn%C3%A9tig_(1723)_(crop).jpg

www.ingramcontent.com/pod-product-compliance
Lightning Source LLC
Chambersburg PA
CBHW072105050526
44107CB00099B/521